Playing
For
Keeps

Biblical Keys to Preservation and Increase

By
Pastor Tim Gilligan

Published by
Ocala Word of Faith Church, Inc.
Additional copies available. Use order form in the back of this book.

CONTENTS

Dedication

I dedicate this book to my friend, my wife, my "*good thing*," Alicia. God didn't call me to walk this road alone and I'm glad He called you to walk with me!

Forward
by Jim and Kathi Kaseman

God is raising up a generation of men and women whom He has called to proclaim the message of faith in God to a lost and dying world. Tim Gilligan is a part of that generation.

Tim is an outstanding Pastor and superb teacher of the Word. Over the past eight years I've watched him mature not only as a minister of the Gospel but in his personal walk with the Lord. His life and ministry exemplify the principles He teaches in this book. God is using Him to be a blessing to the Body of Christ through His strong, yet graceful teaching gift, flowing forth in the Spirit of Truth and Love.

In his book, ***Play For Keeps***, Tim addresses the crucial subject of the believer's responsibility to stand fast and grow up in the things of God. He places emphasis not only on being blessed, but allowing those blessings to cause you to become a blessing to others. In other words, it is time to walk the walk and not just talk the talk!

As you read this book you will receive Biblical keys that will enable you to persevere and live a victorious life in the best of circumstances and in the most adverse situations. This book will challenge you to finish the course that God has set before you and win!

Forward
by Dennis Burke

What is it that makes one person possess the things God has promised, and another person become paralyzed in their ability to progress? Why do some people rise up out of extremely difficult problems and see God sustain them, while others bump along without any significant change?

I believe it is a matter of perspective. One person will focus on the promises of God, while another may focus on their problems and failures.

One of the greatest needs we have today is for powerful and sound teaching from those who have seen for themselves the kind of success the Word of God brings. We not only need to know how to cause God to move in our lives, but also how to *keep* what He provides.

Our society is starving for leaders that will bring genuine answers and stability. That kind of stability comes only from a deep trust in Jesus the Anointed One, and walking in His Word.

God has used Tim Gilligan to raise up a flourishing ministry in Ocala, Florida . His godly leadership and loving guidance---along with very sound teaching---make life rich for those who receive his ministry.

"Playing for Keeps" brings that same enrichment to life. This book is a powerful tool which will lead you into some of the most important aspects found in Scripture---victory and success.

In a fresh way, with his clear and often humorous illustrations, Pastor Tim relates ingredients that can keep you on course to the good life that God has created for you.

1

Preservation and Increase

Did you know that God intended our faith for something more than just receiving? Certainly, we all like to receive, especially when we've been waiting for a long time. But God has a plan to take us from glory to glory, as we move to ever-greater heights in Him.

That plan is for *preservation and increase.* That means we can continue to enjoy the blessing we have received by faith, and then we can see it grow. Because God provides for our preservation and increase, we can declare, "My past is redeemed, my present makes sense, my future is secure." That's good news!

But we have an important part in this plan. God expects us to make up our minds to "play for keeps."

Let's look at Psalm 31: 22, 23.
For I said in my haste, "I am cut off from before Your eyes." Nevertheless You heard the voice of my supplications when I cried out to You. Oh, love the Lord, all you His saints! For the Lord preserves the faithful,...

Some people notice only the part in verse 22 about being cut off before His eyes. But David tells us he said that in his haste. You've probably heard the saying "haste makes waste." What is the opposite of waste? Preservation and increase.

11

There's more to verse 22:

"...Nevertheless You heard the voice of my supplications when I cried out to You."

A beloved Christian song says, "His eye is on the sparrow, so I know He's watching me." Did you know that He is watching you? Now, He is not waiting to see you do something wrong, so He can thump your little head. Yes, God is watching you, but it's because He wants to look after you.

Psalm 34:15, 17 says, *"The eyes of the Lord are on the righteous, and His ears are open to their cry....The righteous cry out, and the Lord hears, and delivers them out of all their troubles."* You're not cut off from before His eyes!

Sometimes in the problems that we face, we'll say, "It just seems like God doesn't see, God doesn't know, God doesn't care! Where is He?" But God does see you, and He is waiting for you to cry out to Him.

Look at verse 23 of Psalm 31: *"Oh, love the Lord, all you His saints! For the Lord preserves the faithful."* The Lord preserves the faithful. The word for "preserve" here means "to guard, to protect, to maintain." Is God able to guard, protect, and maintain? Absolutely.

Now most people live in fear of losing what they have. Many believers and, sadly, many "Word people" live in fear that they will lose what they've gained through faith. They're afraid of losing their healing, or losing their job, or losing their peace. They believe that whatever they do, it is going to fail. But all the while the Bible tells us that if we follow the Word, we'll prosper in whatever we set our hands to do. (Psalm 1:3; Joshua 1:8.)

Preservation and Increase

God gives us healing, but beyond healing, He gives us health. Yet so many people live in the fear of a devastating sickness or injury. The way to dispel that fear is to get back to the Word of God. There you will find over and over that for what God gives you, there is preservation, there is increase, and you can play for keeps.

You don't have to live a life of fear. Have you ever heard these sayings? "This can't last." ... "I wonder when this will get messed up." ... "I'd better enjoy it while it lasts." Or the ever-infamous "All good things must come to an end."

Yet the Bible says, ***"The Lord preserves the faithful."*** God will take care of what He puts in your life. It's not God's plan or design for you to lose it all. Yes, you can mess it up. But He has given us keys to preservation and increase, made clear in multiplied scriptures. If you do these things, God will bring preservation and increase into your life.

We must quit living according to others' fears, others' failures, and others' experiences. Have you had concerns about your health? Probably everybody has. My grandfather, my great-grandfather, and my mother died of cancer. If I go the world's way, I'll think, "I guess it's me next." No, it's not me! That's finished, in my family. I'm standing on the Word of God, and cancer has come this far and goes no further! I'm fully persuaded.

People consider stepping out in a business venture, but they say, "Somebody else did that once, and they failed. I watched them go belly up." Have you ever worried about the economy? There is one major reason for the economic problems throughout all time. Fear!

13

You may say, "No, it's greed." Well what is greed? It is fear. "I've got to get it all now because I might lose it." ... "I have to hide it away." It's like we have heard before, "Get all you can, can all you get and sit on your can." That is what greed is, and that is fear-motivated.

Faith comes by hearing, but so does fear. It's not original with me, but it is truth that the four major causes of recession are ABC, NBC, CBS, and CNN. Sometimes I think the media people drive around in their vans with their cameras, looking only for something discouraging (or perverted) to bring you that night on the news.

So you must quit living your life based on somebody else's fears, failures, and experiences. And further than that, quit using those things to limit God. The only limits on God are the ones *you* place on Him.

The goal of faith is not just to receive. In the '70s, when there was a resurgence of faith teaching, people began to focus on receive, receive, receive. Some called it "Cadillac faith." But that is only partially what faith is about. You receive, but why do you receive? To give. If God can get it *through* you, God will get it *to* you.

We confuse it, because when He gets it to us, we say "Look what I've got." But it's not just for you! I heard a minister say that when God anoints someone, He has someone else in mind. And when He blesses somebody, He has somebody else in mind. The goal is not just to be blessed. It's to be a blessing.

Faith just for receiving is an incomplete faith. Any gift you have, even if it's a cheerful countenance and a happy personality, that's not for you only. It's not so you can stand in front of the mirror and entertain yourself. If God gave you a likable personality, or a fine singing voice, or a way of declaring the Word that commands attention, or any other gift or ability, it's not just for you. Oh, yes, it's for you to enjoy and to use, but it is for others. He has blessed you so that others can benefit.

Let's get beyond just being blessed, to being the blessing. But you can't be a blessing if a blessing came into your life, and you lost it.

"Well, what happened to your healing?"

"I talked myself right out of it." Typically, that's the case. Or you get into disobedience or sin. The focus of this book is not on "if you do this, you will lose what you have received." Instead we will major on the keys to preservation and increase.

Now read this carefully: "The things of God are for your good. And the things of God are yours for good."

When I say they are yours for good, that means *forever*. You may have heard the phrase "bulldog faith." When a bulldog finds a bone, he concentrates on two things. He sniffs that bone, and he looks at it, and he decides: "This bone is good." Then he makes another determination: "This bone is mine." That's what it is about. "This bone is good, and this bone is mine." You can try to take it away from him. But he isn't in a mood to negotiate. He won't let go to talk to you.

See, that's one of the things you must do. The devil will come around trying to talk you out of your blessing. If you lay it down to answer him, you'll wind up saying, "Oh, no! Come back with that!" Hold on to what you have. Don't let go of it. Hold on like that bulldog. Make up your mind, "This bone is good. And this bone is mine."

The things of God are for your good, and the things of God are yours for good. If He gives you healing, He wants you to keep healing. If He gives you peace, He wants you to keep peace. If He works a miracle in your finances, He wants you to keep it. If He gives you victory over a temptation, He wants you to stay victorious over that thing.

In Mark 4:3, Jesus says to the crowd, *"Listen!"*—he wants their close attention— *"Behold, a sower went out to sow."* But His disciples *don't understand* His illustration. He replies, *"Do you not understand this parable? How then will you understand all the parables?"* In verse 14, He explains, *"The sower sows the word."* You must understand this, He is saying. If you don't understand about seed, then how are you going to understand the rest of the parables?

Jesus talks about seed in three different ways in this chapter of Mark, to make sure they get this concept. The sower sows seed, which is the Word. In verse 26, He compares the growth in the kingdom of God to the results of a man's scattering seed. And in verse 30, he tells of the increase from a tiny mustard seed. This is the way the kingdom of God works.

Look at 1 Peter 1:23, 25.
   "Having been born again, not of corruptible seed but incorruptible, through the word of God which lives and abides forever….But the word of the Lord endures forever."

You were born again of incorruptible seed that lives and abides forever. In other words, preservation and increase.

Now what is the seed? The seed is the Word. And the Word does what? It endures forever. So we must base everything in our lives upon the Word. Over every situation, give me the Word, the incorruptible seed that lives and abides forever. The Word of the Lord endures forever.

Back in Mark 4:8, Jesus tells of the power of the Word:
   "But other seed fell on good ground and yielded a crop that sprang up, increased and produced: some thirtyfold, some sixty, and some a hundred."

Look how the seed yielded a crop that sprang up, increased, and produced. Now in the original Greek, Mark used present active participles of these verbs. By this he was emphasizing that each one is a *continuous and repeated action.*

So the Word of God will yield a crop in your life, that will spring up (continuous and repeated action), increase (continuous and repeated action), and produce (continuous and repeated action). That's the way the Word of God works: preservation and increase.

Moving forward to verses 26-29—
   And He said, "The kingdom of God is as if a man should scatter seed on the ground,
   "and should sleep by night and rise by day, and the seed should sprout and grow, he himself does not know how.
   "For the earth yields crops by itself: first the blade, then the head, after that the full grain in the head.
   "But when the grain ripens, immediately he puts in the sickle, because the harvest has come."

17

So here again we see the kingdom of God pictured by a man scattering seed, the seed being the Word of God. He sows the Word, the Word sprouts, the Word grows, it brings forth a crop, and finally there is the harvest. When the Word is planted—that incorruptible seed that lives and abides forever—then things start to sprout up.

When you were first born again, were you just suddenly mature? Have you ever done dumb things as a Christian? We've all done dumb things out of our zeal and out of our lack of knowledge. But the Word says that you should sprout, and I love watching believers sprout. That's a continuous and repeated growth. And we're to grow and to become strong, and we're to keep on growing -- continuous, repeated action. Keep on growing, because you are going to produce a harvest.

Somewhere, somebody planted in *you* the incorruptible seed that lives and abides forever. Then it sprouted and grew, and now you're able to produce seed yourself. Then you can go forth bearing precious seed, and you shall doubtless come again, bringing your sheaves with you. (Psalm 126:6.) And the harvest—now get this—the harvest is the key to future harvests. Harvest ensures the next harvest, because a big part of the harvest is not just for food, but for seed. Preservation and increase.

In verses 30-32 of Mark 4, Jesus brings the third parable about seed. He is saying,

"I'm going to get this across to you, one way or the other."

Then He said,

"To what shall we liken the kingdom of God? Or with what parable shall we picture it?

"It is like a mustard seed which, when it is sown on the ground, is smaller than all the seeds on earth;

"but when it is sown, it grows up and becomes greater than all herbs, and shoots out large branches, so that the birds of the air may nest under its shade."

It becomes a tree; it becomes a huge tree. It grows and becomes great. It provides benefits for others. You're to provide benefits for others. You're not just to stay a seed. You're not just to stay a sprout. You're to develop into a tree, one with branches that can provide rest and shade for others.

Now let's look at some other verses pertaining to trees.

He shall be like a tree planted by the rivers of water that brings forth its fruit in its season, whose leaf also shall not wither, and whatever he does shall prosper.
Psalm 1:3

Blessed is the man who trusts in the Lord,...
Jeremiah 17:7

Do you trust the Lord? Well if you do, you're blessed. Quit saying, "Oh, it's just pitiful, it's horrible." Instead you should say, "You know, I'm blessed. Yes, anybody can see this is messed up. But I'm blessed, because I trust the Lord. Romans 10:11 tells me that if I trust the Lord I will not be disappointed, and Jeremiah 17:7 says that I am blessed."
...And whose hope is the Lord.
For he shall be like a tree planted by the waters, Which spreads out its roots by the river, And will not fear when heat comes; But its leaf will be green, And will not be

anxious in the year of drought, Nor will cease from yielding fruit.

Jeremiah 17:7-8

Why doesn't he fear when heat comes? Because he has his roots spread out by the river. Quit looking at all the outside; get some roots. You have nothing to fear. Remember, you're blessed if you trust in the Lord.

"... Nor will cease from yielding fruit." Doesn't that sound like preservation and increase to you?

In Isaiah 61:3 we read—

To console those who mourn in Zion, To give them beauty for ashes, The oil of joy for mourning, The garment of praise for the spirit of heaviness; That they may be called trees of righteousness, The planting of the Lord, that He may be glorified.

"... Trees of righteousness, the planting of the Lord." Have you ever looked at those little discount-store trees? The store workers keep each one in a bucket, bring them out every day, and set them in front, so maybe somebody will buy them. Just like those trees, some people have great potential to grow and flourish in the kingdom of God, but nothing's happening. I've learned that no roots means no fruit. You've got to get planted. You've got to get some stability. Get out of your bucket and sink down some roots by rivers of living water.

When the wind comes, the discount-store tree in its bucket gets knocked over. But when you are the planting of the Lord, you've got roots, you've got strength. If the wind blows, you can just let it cool you off. You're growing, and you're becoming strong and great. But you've got to get planted. Some people are so used to saying, "Oh, the wind is blowing; time for me to pull up roots." You just stay there, just stay planted. But first get planted.

"... The planting of the Lord that He may be glorified." My father-in-law planted some young fruit trees—orange, lime, peach, apple, and cherry. He's not trying to start an orchard; he just wants to have these trees. He's planted one or two of each in different places on his property. He drives his little tractor around to go water those trees.

When he planted them a few years ago, he wasn't really "glorified." They were just skinny, bare saplings. If visitors came, he didn't take them over and say, "This is our peach tree," because it just looked like a stick. Then a year or so later, it bore two little peaches for the first time. They weren't edible, and my daughter pulled them off to see, before my father-in-law got to be glorified in his peaches.

We read about these trees of righteousness. Their leaf is green, they produce fruit, they're rooted and strong, and, it says, in that the Father is glorified. Not in dormant little twigs. If you're just standing there, the Father is not glorified in that. We're to be constantly growing, blooming, bearing, and providing fruit, rest and shade for others.

John 15:8 says,
"By this My Father is glorified, that you bear much fruit; ..."

That's what glorifies the Father. It's like my father-in-law's trees. My wife and I talk about it virtually every time we pull onto his property. We see those trees, and every month they're getting

21

a little bigger and a little stronger. In years to come, they will be big, big trees. Certain times of the year, we'll be able to pick cherries off one, apples off another, and limes off another. Then my father-in-law will tell visitors, "Come on over and let's get you a peach right off my tree."

What glorifies the Father God is when you bear much fruit. No wonder there hasn't been harvest out of a lot of people and a lot of churches, because they're just standing there barren and saying, "You know, if you get born again, you can be just like me." So folks run back into the world fast, because who wants to be like that? Be a tree that gets planted and stays planted. Draw from the soil and draw from the river. Bear much fruit and glorify the Father!

Romans 1:16 says,
"For I am not ashamed of the gospel of Christ, for it is the power of God to salvation."

That word "salvation" in the Greek is *sozo*, and it means deliverance or rescue, safety, healing, soundness, and (are you ready?) preservation.

Have you ever had a need? Well, what you must do with that need is to find seed. You must find a promise for the provision, in the Word of God. By faith in that promise you receive the manifestation, and the need is met. We have it, but we've not learned how to keep it. We've not learned to walk in preservation and increase. That's the purpose of this book.

What God provides does not wear out. What God provides does not break. What God provides does not go out of style. His promises do not grow less or decrease, and they do not expire. You are not going to wake up some day and go to pray, and get a notice, "Sorry, God's no longer in business."

One time before I was married, a man at church told me, "Hey, this fitness center is having a tremendous sale. You can join for $50 for the year." And he said, "It's a great place." So I paid my $50, and I went once. That afternoon I bought some new shorts and a gym bag and sweat bands—all the "stuff." I went back the next day, and there was nothing in the building, nothing! Not even my $50. Out of business and out of town.

God is not like that. He is going to be there! He sees, and He knows, and He is able to do something about it. God says, "I know what to do. Let Me do it." And God will take care of it. And what God gives you doesn't break.

God is not going to embarrass you. When I was in the sixth grade, my aunt sent me some pants. I hated those pants. They looked funny, and they didn't fit. I tried to hide them. I'd be wearing the old jeans that I liked, and my mom would say, "Wait, young man. Here are those pants your aunt got for you. Put these on."

"No, Mom, no."

"There's nothing wrong with these pants. Here, you go put these pants on." And I'd go put them on. I'd go off to school embarrassed. But God won't do that to you. He'll give you a custom fit. He's able to take care of you and do it right, and it's going to last and be a blessing!

The greatest quality of God is His faithfulness. He's your healer. But what if He wasn't faithful? He's your peace. But what if He

23

wasn't faithful? "Yes, He's your peace, but He's off today." No, God doesn't take a day off. He is there all the time.

He's promised to meet our material needs. He has all the wealth. He has everything that He needs to provide for you, but what if He wasn't faithful? You see, the greatest quality of God is that He is faithful. He's everything to us, and in being everything, He's faithful. Aren't you glad for that?

God took care of the children of Israel. He gave them shoes that didn't go out of style and didn't wear out, for forty years! He led them with fire by night and a cloud by day. He gave them manna in the morning. He brought water out of the rocks when they were thirsty. He took care of them. The day they left Egypt, the scripture clearly says, there was none feeble among them, there was no sickness among them. God is faithful. God will take care of you. He is completely able to take care of you.

John 10:10 says,
"The thief does not come except to steal, and to kill, and to destroy."

You know the devil has nothing except what he can get from you. Remember how some kids at school were all the time "bumming" at lunch? "Can I have your roll?" ... "Can I have your chocolate milk?" There might even be one guy who diverted your attention, and if you turned for a minute, he took what was yours.

But through our understanding and applying the promises of God, and by utilizing the keys discussed in this book, we can experience and live in preservation and increase. It is time for us to learn how to play for keeps.

2
For Your Good, Yours For Good

Jesus Christ is the same yesterday, today, and forever.
Hebrews 13:8

Forever, O Lord, Your word is settled in heaven.
Psalm 119:89

The Word of God is not valid one day and out of date the next. It's not like your car insurance. You get it paid off, you feel good about it, you forget about it, and then you get a renewal notice in the mail. The promises of God and the value of the Word of God do not fade away. His Word is forever the same.

When you wake up tomorrow, you might not feel very good or very spiritual, but the Word of God is just as true. Feelings have the least to do with it. Once you grasp that truth, your feelings will line up with the truth a whole lot quicker.

If the doctor diagnoses you with something, invariably there is this long line of people descended from Job's comforters. They'll find their way to you and say, "Bless your heart, I knew somebody else that had that same thing." They come sharing all kinds of doom and gloom. Run them out of your yard!

We've got to quit living off the fear of others, the failures of others, the experiences of others. We must quit limiting God on the basis of what happened in somebody else's life. No matter what happens, the bottom line is that God did not fail, and His promises did not fail.

However, some want to challenge that. "Well, Grandma loved God, and Grandma served God." Then they'll suggest, "God smushed her." God did not smush Grandma. We are quicker to defend Grandma than God. We're more willing to stand up for our traditions than we are to ascribe to the truth, which is that God never fails, and His Word never fails.

When I was single, I was "Mr. Microwave." I'd spend at least $90 every time I went to the grocery store just for me, because it was all microwave food. I didn't have much of anything in the refrigerator. It was all in the freezer. I was visiting a family one day for dinner. The wife was a real "coupon lady," and she gave me some coupons. She told me Thursday was the best day to shop, so I cut out the coupons and put them on my kitchen counter, with great intentions.

A couple of months later I remembered them. I decided to be a good steward, and so I went to the grocery store. I picked out some things just because I had the coupons. I didn't want them really, I didn't need them, but the coupons made them a good deal. When I was checking out, I asked the cashier, "Do you want these coupons now?" She said, "No, wait until I get all through, and then I'll subtract them." But when I gave her the coupons, she said, "Sir, these are all expired."

God's promises are not that way. If you go before God with a need, you will never hear, "I'm sorry, that promise is no good anymore. It has expired. He won't give you peace in the middle of the night. He won't heal your body anymore. He won't give you favor or wisdom in your situation." Aren't you glad that the Word of God never expires?

The goal of faith is not just to receive. The goal of faith is to receive, and then to have it *preserved,* and then to have it *increase.* That's God's plan of preservation and increase. The goal is not just to get blessed, the goal is to be a blessing, but you can't be a blessing unless you're blessed. When a blessing comes in your life, it is not so you can stack it all around you and say, "Boy, look how blessed I am." No, it comes into your life so that you can be a blessing. That's the plan of God for us.

Remember, "The things of God are for your good; the things of God are yours for good." Think about that—for your family, your business, your health, provision, peace, favor, protection. Those things that God gives you are for your good, and they're yours for good. This is incredibly good news. Take hold of it.

Psalm 34:8 says, "Oh, taste and see that the Lord is good." We learn that by experiencing His blessings. The things of God are good. Healing is good. Peace is good. Victory is good. Remember the bulldog? You need to determine that *this is good and this is mine.* You've got to clench your teeth on that thing. Like the bulldog, don't let go of what you got.

Have you ever played marbles? When I was in school, it was a status symbol to have a sock full of marbles tied to your belt. We played at every opportunity. If we were waiting outside in line to go to the cafeteria, and the line wasn't moving fast enough, and there was dirt right there, we would play.

One time my friend and I decided nothing much was going on in class. This lesson really wasn't going to affect our lives. I thought marbles would liven it up, so I asked the teacher to excuse me to go to the restroom. She said, "OK, hurry back." I had my marbles, and our plan was that my friend was going to meet me. About the time I got to the door, he raised his hand to see if he could go. Unfortunately my marbles kind of jangled right then, and the teacher canceled the tournament.

But when we would play, it didn't matter if it was the other kid's best marble— it didn't matter if it was his grandpa's marble that had been passed down through the family. You drew a circle and you played for keeps. If you knocked his marble out of the circle, it was yours! He might beg, bargain, and try to steal, but it was yours. We called that *playing for keeps.* Once we gain these things in our lives, let's play for keeps.

God's plan and God's will are for preservation and increase, not for things just to come into your life and then suddenly be gone. God brings them into your life for your good, and they are yours for good. But as He brings them, they should be preserved, and they should also be increased, because God's plan is for you to go from glory to glory.

A brother told me, "Pastor, I've found these keys work concerning preservation and increase, but I also found they work for *restoration*."

I believe that is very important too. Have you lost things that you know God has brought into your life? The Holy Spirit is saying, "Get back into the things of God, get back into the flow, and use these keys." God is pleased—He is excited—to bring restoration into your life. The very same keys that will produce preservation and increase will also cause *restoration*.

3

An Attitude of Gratitude

The first key is *being thankful*. You're to have an "attitude of gratitude." This is possibly the single most important key to keeping the things that God brings into your life, because it keeps you focused on God. When we are focused on God, we'll remember that He is our source. It is when we get our attention on the gifts, rather than on the gift giver, that we get enamored and distracted with them, and we lose our focus.

You know, there are some blessings that I honestly believe God can't bring into some of our lives yet, because we couldn't handle it. We must be careful. Remember Third John 2 says that He prospers you as your soul prospers. So first you need to prosper your soul, then God can trust you with it. God will bless you as much as He can. Did you realize that? All the time, God will bless you as much as He can. So be thankful.

A few years back, I was sitting in a dentist chair. A wood plaque on the wall read, "Floss only the teeth you wish to keep." Think about that. Floss only the teeth you wish to keep. Well, the next day when I got in front of the mirror, I didn't pick just one tooth to floss. I did them all. Let's translate this over into our spiritual lives. *Only thank God for the things you wish to keep.*

Ingratitude is the last step before rebellion. Parents, remember that and teach it to your children. Ingratitude is the last step before rebellion. If you have ever rebelled in your life—against your parents, against authority, against God—I guarantee you the last step before that rebellion was a reluctance to be appreciative.

Another principle is that rules without relationship lead to rebellion. What religion did for so many years was just give us rules—rules, rules, rules. There is no life or blessing in coming to church to sit and listen to rules, void of relationship. *Relationship* is what makes the difference. Yes, God gives us rules. But it is relationship with Him that causes us to want to please Him and not to rebel against Him.

Ingratitude is the last step before rebellion, because we lose our focus. We think that we just do what we want, when we want, however we want. We lose our focus completely on God. And so gratitude is a very important thing.

Romans 1: 21, 22 reads—
Because, although they knew God, they did not glorify Him as God, nor were thankful, but became futile in their thoughts, and their foolish hearts were darkened.
Professing to be wise, they became fools.

In the Amplified Bible, it reads—
Because when they knew and recognized Him as God, they did not honor and glorify Him as God or give Him thanks. But instead they became futile and godless in their thinking [with vain imaginings, foolish reasoning, and stupid speculations] and their senseless minds were darkened.
Claiming to be wise, they became fools [professing to be smart, they made simpletons of themselves].

Let's look at this process. They knew God, they recognized God, but they stopped glorifying Him as God or giving Him thanks.

Thanksgiving helps you to stay in the fear of the Lord. My definition of the fear of the Lord is, "A constant response *from* me to God as God, which allows a constant response *to* me from God as God."

Fear of the Lord isn't thinking that He's going to pinch your head off if you do something wrong. It's having such intense love and such deep respect for God, that your greatest dread is of bringing displeasure to Him. And so you are constantly responding to Him as God. You glorify Him as God in every situation.

When you do that, the result is automatic. He responds back to you constantly as God in your life. Isn't that wonderful?

Now, they knew God, and they recognized Him, but they did not glorify Him as God, nor were they thankful. It says that their minds became futile, or their thoughts became vain. That phrase "became vain," or "became futile," in the Greek means "to get off the right path." There are people who have wound up in the ditch. They knew God, they were on the right path, but they stopped glorifying God as God and being thankful to Him.

People get to the point where they think they're smart. The Bible says they become fools. The dangerous thing about this is that it's not a long process. This morning you could say, "I'm thankful," and this afternoon become a fool. How? In any situation, stop glorifying God as God. Stop being thankful, and the next thing you know, you're in the ditch.

31

It says that they professed to be wise, but they became fools. The Amplified Bible says it was because they became godless in their thinking. Psalm 14:1 and Psalm 53:1 declare, ***"The fool has said in his heart, 'There is no God.'"*** Is it possible for somebody to know God, to be a believer on his way to heaven, but be a fool? Yes!

Now this person doesn't go around saying out loud, "I'm a fool," and saying, "There is no God." Where does he say it? He says it *in his heart.*

Proverbs 4:23 tells us that all the issues of life spring from your heart. Even if you're born-again and Spirit-filled, you can say with your actions and with your life, "There is no God." You've become godless in your thinking, not glorifying God as God or thanking Him as God. You'll get off the right path, and your thoughts will become darkened. You'll think that you're on your way to somewhere, but you're actually over here in the ditch.

It doesn't take miles and miles for you to end up in the ditch. It just takes a second, doesn't it? You're driving along, and suddenly you get over into the gravel. Then you clip a few mail boxes, and there you are, up in somebody's yard or over in the ditch.

So you've got to guard yourself in this area by being thankful. Say it aloud, "I'm thankful."

The Bible says in Proverbs 10:14,
> ***"...The mouth of the foolish is near destruction."***

Think about it. If you have said in your heart there is no God, you have become a fool. So remember, we are after preservation and increase, but destruction is always near a fool.

God has a covering for us, but if you choose to come out from under that covering, you are ignoring God. You're ignoring what God says, you're ignoring what God has done in your life, and you think that you're doing it all yourself. In that case, you're over here in the ditch, and you're on your own. You're wide open for attack and everything else.

Now, without being thankful, you'll forget your source. You must be thankful and acknowledge your source. That is the essence of humility. Humility is not bad posture. Humility is a great strength, a great virtue. It is a great power in your life, because whatever comes along, you seek God in it. You're focused on your source.

The Bible says in James 4:6 that God resists—He sets Himself against—the proud, but He gives grace to the humble. Perhaps you have a situation right now that would require some grace. Humble yourself. When you humble yourself, it releases grace.

But if you're going into the presence of God, and you think you've got it together, that you've done it all, that's pride. Satan wasn't kicked out of heaven for smoking. It was pride. It was a form of insanity called pride.

First Corinthians 4:7 asks three questions.
"For who makes you differ from another? And what do you have that you did not receive? Now if you did indeed receive it, why do you boast as if you had not received it?"

Let's break this down by looking at each of these questions. First, "Who makes you differ from another?" Is God a respecter of persons? Of course not. My wife and I consider ourselves so blessed. We've got a wonderful marriage, beautiful children, and a nice home. We've got a wonderful church. Many different kinds of blessing come our way, and we always say, "God loves us the most." We know we're joking, but we really feel this way. And other people say, "No, I'm His favorite."

Every believer should have such a relationship with God. Remember, He can't keep His eyes off you. You should feel as though God's outpouring is on you, but really you are no different from anybody else. God always blesses each of his children as much as He can bless. If you will stay in the right posture, God will bless you. So who makes you differ from another? You are not different from anybody.

Look at the second question. "What do you have that you did not receive?" Think about it. Are you healthy today because you take vitamins? God gave you health. You have sight today. Eating carrots may have helped you, but who gave you the sight? Who gave you the carrots?

If you're good in business, you might think, "I have business savvy." You couldn't even spell *savvy* if it weren't for God. But what do you have that you did not receive? "Well, I made wise choices." Who gave you the wisdom? "I was in the right place at the right time." Who orders your steps? What do you have that you did not receive?

Consider the third question. "Now if you did indeed receive it, why do you boast as if you did not receive it?" If you boast as if you did not receive it, you are becoming godless in your thinking. You will stop glorifying God as God, you will become ungrateful to Him, and you will become futile or vain in your thoughts. That means you'll get off the right path. You'll end up as a fool. And what does Proverbs 10:14 say? Destruction is always near a fool.

The goal here is preservation and increase. How can you avoid all of that? By being thankful. *Be thankful.*

James 1:17 says,
>   *"Every good gift and every perfect gift is from above, and comes down from the Father of lights, with whom there is no variation or shadow of turning."*

Every good thing, every perfect thing in your life came from God.

The 20th Century New Testament says it this way: **"... *Who is Himself never subject to change."* Isn't that something? The Phillips translation says, *"... with whom there is never the slightest variation or shadow of inconsistency."* With God there is never the slightest variation or shadow of inconsistency. He is the same.

That's why your past is redeemed, and your present makes sense, and your future is secure. It is because He never changes, He loves you, and He is not a respecter of persons. He wants to bless you as much as He can bless you, and He wants to preserve those blessings in your life. But we must cooperate with the plan of God.

Deuteronomy 8:10-11 says,
>   *"When you have eaten and are full, then you shall bless the Lord your God for the good land which He has given you. Beware..."*

If you are going swimming, and a sign says "Beware," followed by some small print, wouldn't you want to know what the small print says? It might say piranhas are in the pool. You might just assume, "Oh, it means don't dive." No matter how much you avoid diving, the piranhas are going to have you for lunch.

So let's read what the "beware" is, in verses 11-17.

> *Beware that you do not forget the Lord your God by not keeping His commandments, His judgments, His statutes which I command you today,*
>
> *lest when you have eaten and are full or satisfied and have built beautiful houses and dwell in them;*
>
> *and when your herds and flocks multiply, and when your silver and gold are multiplied, and all that you have is multiplied;*
>
> *when your heart is lifted up and you forget the Lord your God who brought you out of the land of Egypt, from the house of bondage;*
>
> *who led you through that great and terrible wilderness, in which were fiery serpents and scorpions and thirsty land where there was no water; who brought water for you out of the flinty rock;*
>
> *who fed you in the wilderness with manna, which your fathers did not know, that He might humble you and that He might test you, to do you good in the end—*
>
> *then you say in your heart, "My power and the might of my hand have gained me this wealth."*

Now Moses is talking here to Israel, but the same thing applies to any of us. When we get to the point where our business is prospering or our family is thriving, and we're feeling good, there is a tendency to think, "I'm doing pretty well." We go on our way doing our thing, and we forget God's part in it.

Verse 14 says that your heart gets lifted up. The way that your heart gets lifted up is when your mind gets out of place. Your thoughts become darkened. You get off the right path. Then your heart gets puffed up with pride, and you think that you have accomplished something.

But notice this in verse 18.
   "And you shall remember the Lord your God, for it is He who gives you power to get wealth, that He may establish His covenant which He swore to your fathers, as it is this day."

The key here is thankfulness!

How am I not going to forget the Lord? By thanking Him for everything that He does for me. Everything that I have, I've received. I received it from the Father of lights, with whom there is no variation neither shadow of turning—not even the slightest hint of inconsistency. I got it from God, because He loves me. Now did He give it to me so I would lose it? Did He give it to me because it is not going to last anyway? No. God brought it into my life to bless me with it and so that I might be a blessing with it.

Psalm 100:4 declares, *"Enter into His gates with thanksgiving."* Now you must enter with thanksgiving. That is the only way that you can enter. So our focus must be on thanksgiving. When you come into the presence of God, even if you are coming in a time of need, the Bible says in Hebrews 4:16 you can come boldly.

But why are you coming boldly? Because you acknowledge and you are thankful that you have access by faith, and you know you can have that confidence—because of the blood of Jesus. You receive that, you acknowledge that, you thank Him for that. It makes you eligible to go in and partake of His grace and mercy and goodness.

It says, ***"Enter into His gates with thanksgiving, And into His courts with praise."*** Praise is actually for what He has done. The word "bless" in the Hebrew means "to bend the knee." What is that? To humble yourself. What is to humble yourself? To acknowledge Him as your source.

Let's add verse 5.
> *Enter into His gates with thanksgiving,*
> *And into His courts with praise.*
> *Be thankful to Him and bless His name,*
> *For the Lord is good;*
> *His mercy is everlasting,*
> *And His truth endures to all generations.*

Thanksgiving puts you in remembrance, and thanksgiving keeps you in remembrance. Thanksgiving puts your focus right, thanksgiving keeps your focus right—on God.

Thankfulness is one of the keys to keeping what God has given you. Its effect is that you don't become distracted by what you have, but you know where it came from, and why He blessed you with it. Remember, if He blessed you with anything, even getting born again, it wasn't completely just for you. You were born again so someone else could get born again. If he healed your body, it wasn't just so that you would feel better. It's actually for someone else's benefit, too.

God is so efficient. He never does anything that has only one purpose. Even if He does it in secret, it will create in you a faith and a confidence and an assurance that will have an effect on other people's lives. God desires to bless you, and God desires for you to hold onto that blessing and see it increase.

Just for a minute, let's look at Christian etiquette. I believe that Christians should have etiquette. They should shine. If you're at a restaurant having fellowship or an important business lunch, when the waitress brings you a glass of water, don't ignore her. Look up and say, "Thank you." You sow into other people's lives. Say thank you.

One day I was in a restaurant, and I couldn't see myself, but I knew that I had bleu cheese dressing on my mouth. The waitress came up and refilled my tea, and I used a napkin to wipe my face, because it's hard to take a compliment from a guy who has stuff all over his face. She was waiting to see if I wanted something extra, but I said, "I just wanted to say, 'Thank you.'"

She said "Oh, you're welcome." It is not just so you can get good service the rest of the meal. It is proper etiquette.

Men, if your wife does something for you, if she brings you some tea, if she cooks you a meal, thank her. Ladies, your husband may not be president of IBM, but if he's out there doing a job, you might encourage him to do a better job by showing your appreciation when he comes home.

When your children make an effort to do the right thing, thank them. My son will try to make his bed. Well, at least the bedspread is on top. But we don't say, "You call this making a bed?" No, we thank him. We encourage him. You should be sowing into other people's lives. You should thank others.

You should thank people who help you at church. I watch the ushers that open doors so people can get back to their babies, and I see the dedicated nursery workers and children's workers that made it possible for parents to enjoy the service. You need to thank them. We need to be thankful for one another.

We need to be most thankful to God. You must get the revelation of thanksgiving. It should be most of the praying that you do. When I go to bed at night, I don't beg God, "Please protect us, oh please, protect us." No, we put the children to bed and I thank God.

I say "Thank You, Lord, that You have promised to protect us. That protection belongs to us because we are redeemed. Thank You, Lord, that You have given Your angels charge over us, to keep us in all our ways. Thank You, Lord, that no evil will befall us, nor shall any plague come near our dwelling. Thank You that Your Word said that we can lie down unafraid and that You give Your beloved sweet sleep."

If I bring you a gift meant especially for you, you don't have to beg for it, you just reach out. Then it is proper, when you receive something, to say thank you. We are people of faith, so when God offers and extends all His provision to us, *faith says, "Thank you."*

Now this is a key, and I pray that you'll put it on your spiritual key ring. *Be thankful.* In your prayer time, thank Him for His promises. Don't beg Him for His promises. That's an insult to God. He paid such a dear price to get it to you. He got it right there to you, and you're begging for it, and you turn around and walk away because you didn't *feel* something. Thank Him for it. That's the evidence you've received it.

Why don't you right now take a few moments to be thankful? Out loud, begin to thank the Lord. Thank Him for your job. If you're thinking, "Well, I don't like my job," thank Him that you have a job. Be faithful on that job, because promotion comes from the Lord. Thank the Lord for your health. Maybe your response is "Well, I'm not feeling too good." Thank Him for what you do have, and thank Him that He's the healer.

Thanksgiving is a major key.

4

It's Time to Listen

T he second key to playing for keeps is *listening.* Proverbs
1:32, 33 reads,
   *"For the turning away of the simple will slay them, And
the complacency of fools will destroy them; But whoever
listens to me will dwell safely, And will be secure, without
fear of evil."*

We are studying about preservation and increase, about playing
for keeps. We don't want destruction in our lives. We don't want
our efforts to be slain and to be terminated. We don't want that to
happen. The scripture speaks very clearly. We must listen.

This passage shows us that the turning away of the simple will
slay them. That phrase *turning away* in the Hebrew is
"backsliding." It is the backsliding of the simple. They were on the
right track, but they turned away.

In Joshua 1:7, God warned against going to the left or the right
of what He had said. Proverbs 4:26, 27 says,
   *"Ponder the path of your feet, And let all your ways be
established. Do not turn to the right or the left; Remove
your foot from evil."*

So you are to go straight ahead. Carefully consider where your
steps are taking you. Don't turn away from that path of life.

We saw in Romans 1:21 that when you become ungrateful, your mind and your thoughts become futile. We saw that the Greek word for *futile* meant "to turn aside to the wrong path." So here in Proverbs 1:32 the simple person has also turned away from the right path, to veer onto a course that will slay him.

The next phrase of Proverbs 1:32 says, ***"And the complacency of fools will destroy them."*** These are the fools who said in their hearts, "There is no God." These are the unthankful ones who professed to be wise but became fools. Now a dangerous complacency has set in. The word *complacency* here means "careless ease."

God wants to put you in a place of ease, but not careless ease. You have to continue to do the things that got you to that point of ease. On the morning after the battle, you'd better be as sharp as you were the day before. Otherwise, the enemy comes right back and snatches away what you took from him, and more besides. So you must persevere in the things that brought you to that victory.

Verse 33 shows how to defend against the enemy. ***"But whoever listens to me will dwell safely,..."*** Look at the result of listening. Wouldn't you like to dwell safely? Now look at this: "... And will be secure, without fear of evil." In the margin of my Bible it says *secure* means "at ease"—not careless ease, but at ease.

The scripture says that you can dwell safely, you can be at ease, and you can be without fear of evil. All of that comes from listening.

The Hebrew word *shama,* translated here as *listen,* means "to hear intelligently, to give attention and obedience." There is a big difference between just hearing and listening. What we must do is learn to listen. That means not just to give ear, not just to give attention, but also to give obedience. In James 1:22 we read,

"But be doers of the word, and not hearers only, deceiving yourselves."

If you just hear something, and you don't act upon it, you are deceiving yourself. Even if you give the Word of God attention, but you don't give it obedience, you are fooling yourself.

Now where does all deception come from? The devil. In John 8:44, Jesus calls him the father of lies. All deceit, all deception comes from the devil, and so if we are deceiving ourselves by hearing and not doing, we are cooperating with the devil's plan for our lives. When you hear and you don't do, you are cooperating with the devil's plan for your life.

The devil's next move, now that disobedience has opened you up to doubting the truth, is to try to discredit the Word of God. He says, "Look, you heard that sermon, you even bought the tape, you even took notes. And it didn't do anything for you." He comes to slander God's Word. You have cooperated with the devil's plan for your life, which was to deceive you so that he can steal the Word from you. Don't deceive yourself by being a hearer only, but be a doer!

James 1:23-25 continues—

For if anyone is a hearer of the word and not a doer, he is like a man observing his face in a mirror;

for he observes himself, goes away, and immediately forgets what kind of man he was.

But he who looks into the perfect law of liberty and continues in it, and is not a forgetful hearer but a doer of the work, this one will be blessed in what he does.

Now in order to be a blessing, you must be blessed, and if you want to be blessed, you must not be a forgetful hearer, but a doer. When we hear the things of the Word of God, we must not just take time out and give our ear, we must give our hearts too, and let it result in action.

There is a difference between hearing and listening. You can be praying to God or reading His Word, and you're going through the motions, but you may not be listening. Your heart isn't open to hear anything. When it comes to hearing from God, you need to be still and know that He is God. (Psalm 46:10.).

First Samuel 3:2-10 tells how Samuel is awakened in the night. When he realizes that what he hears is the voice of the Lord, he says, ***"Speak, for Your servant listens."*** It's the Hebrew word *shama* again. Listening must be an attitude that says, "I'm ready to hear, and I'm ready to do." That's the way we need to be with the Lord.

In the books of Matthew, Mark, Luke, and Revelation, we find the phrase, "He who has ears, let him hear." Hebrews 3:15 says, ***"Today, if you will hear His voice."***

Everything that He would say would be wisdom to us. First Timothy 1:17 and Jude 25 call God the one "who alone is wise." One of the seven spirits of God named in Isaiah 11:2 is the spirit of wisdom.

In Proverbs 8:1-5, the voice of wisdom cries aloud. Where is that coming from? It is coming from God. Wisdom cries aloud. But we have to listen for it.

Does not wisdom cry out, And understanding lift up her voice?

She takes her stand on the top of the high hill, Beside the way, where the paths meet.

She cries out by the gates, at the entry of the city, At the entrance of the doors: "To you, O men, I call, And my voice is to the sons of men.

O you simple ones, understand prudence, And you fools, be of an understanding heart."

Verse 32 uses the word *shama* in connection with receiving wisdom. Certainly, listening is a key to preservation and increase.

Now therefore, listen to me, my children, For blessed are those who keep my ways.

Hear instruction and be wise, And do not disdain it.

Blessed is the man who listens to me, watching daily at my gates, waiting at the post of my doors.

For whoever finds me finds life, And obtains favor from the Lord.

In Proverbs 9:1, wisdom is again seeking those who will listen, inviting them to enjoy the benefits of living wisely.

Wisdom has built her house, She has hewn out her seven pillars;

She has slaughtered her meat, She has mixed her wine, She has also furnished her table.

She has sent out her maidens, she cries out from the highest places of the city.

"Whoever is simple, let him turn in here!" As for him who lacks understanding, she says to him,

> *"Come, eat of my bread And drink of the wine I have mixed.*
> *Forsake foolishness and live, And go in the way of understanding..."*

However, in Proverbs 9:13-18, someone else is crying out. It is not wisdom, but "a foolish woman." In the scriptures, this woman is the harlot or the immoral seductress, who represents anything that pulls you away or distracts you from God. It can be chocolate, it can be sports, it can be a boat, it can be friends, or it can be some activity that you're involved in.

> *A foolish woman is clamorous; She is simple and knows nothing.*
> *For she sits at the door of her house, On a seat by the highest places of the city, To call to those who pass by, Who go straight on their way:*
> *"Whoever is simple, let him turn in here"; And as for him who lacks understanding, she says to him,*
> *"Stolen water is sweet, And bread eaten in secret is pleasant."*
> *But he does not know that the dead are there, That her guests are in the depths of hell.*

We see here that we must be careful what we listen to and make sure that it is the voice of God, and not one turning you away from the right path. Proverbs 4:20 cautions,

> *"My son, give attention to my words; Incline your ear to my sayings."*

In Matthew 7:24, 25, Jesus explains the importance of giving attention and obedience to His words.

Therefore whoever hears these sayings of Mine, and does them, I will liken him to a wise man that built his house on a rock:

and the rain descended, the floods came, the winds blew and beat on that house; and it did not fall, for it was founded on the rock.

Now let me point this out about preservation and increase. It does not mean that problems will not come. Problems will come. Jesus said in John 16:33, from the Amplified Bible,

I have told you these things, so that in Me you may have [perfect] peace and confidence. In the world you have tribulation and trials and distress and frustration; but be of good cheer [take courage; be confident, certain, undaunted]! For I have overcome the world. [I have deprived it of power to harm you and have conquered it for you.]

He told us to expect tribulation, trials, distress, and frustration in this world. Now look at this fellow in the house. The rain descended, the floods came, the winds blew, they beat on his house. But it did not fall. Why? It was founded on the rock.

What about his neighbor just across the street? They go to the same church—sometimes they car pool together. When the storm comes, they experience the same attack. (Matthew 7:26, 27.)

But everyone who hears these sayings of Mine, and does not do them, will be like a foolish man who built his house on the sand:

and the rain descended, the floods came, and the winds blew and beat on that house; and it fell. And great was its fall.

What is the difference between these two men? The one built his house on a rock, the other built his house on sand. What makes the difference? They went to the same church. Both of them heard the same sermons. Both of them had the same daily devotional. Both of them had Jesus T-shirts.

Both of them had all the "stuff," but one of them listened, he heard, and he obeyed. He established the foundation and structure of his life upon a rock, and that protected him. The same things came against both of them. The same things come against everybody.

The Bible says in First Corinthians 10:13, *"No temptation has overtaken you except such as is common to man."* You're not like the little character who walks around with a black cloud over his head, while everyone else is in the sunshine. It rains on the just and the unjust alike.

Whatever comes, what really matters is how you're able to withstand it. It was the same storm, but the man who built on the rock didn't lose anything. If anything, he gained a house guest: the guy from across the street. We must listen. We must hear. We must do.

Proverbs 19:27 reminds us,
> *"Cease listening to instruction, my son, And you will stray from the words of knowledge."*

Proverbs 5:7, 8 bears this out.
> *Therefore hear me now, my children, And do not depart from the words of my mouth.*
> *Remove your way far from her, And do not go near the door of her house.*

We are talking about this foolish woman again, who symbolizes anything that pulls you away from God. The principle is this: it is better to go the long way than the wrong way.

In verses 9-13 we see the consequences of straying from the words of knowledge. Does this sound like preservation and increase here?

> *Lest you give your honor to others, And your years to the cruel one;*
>
> *Lest aliens be filled with your wealth, And your labors go to the house of a foreigner;*
>
> *And you mourn at last when your flesh and your body are consumed,*
>
> *And say, "How, I have hated instruction, And my heart despised correction!*
>
> *I have not obeyed the voice of my teachers, Nor inclined my ear to those who instructed me!"*

Verse 14 tells the final outcome.

> *"I was on the verge of total ruin, In the midst of the assembly and congregation."*

The choice is yours. The key here is listening to God. Let me point this out, however, don't worry about setting your ear to try to hear the voice of God. Some people get so "woo woo" about it.

The Holy Spirit will speak to you, but He will speak to you through the Word first. Start by spending time in the Word. As you get versed in it and familiar with it, then God can speak to your heart. Jesus said in John 14:26 the Spirit would bring all His words to our remembrance.

So you must load yourself with the Word and give it your full attention. Let God lead you with His Word.

Let's read Proverbs 1:33 one more time. *"Whoever listens to me will dwell safely, And will be secure, without fear of evil."* Give your attention and obedience to the Word, and you will live in God's protection, guidance, and peace.

5
Walking In Wisdom

T he next key is to *walk in wisdom.* Let me paraphrase for you exactly what that means: *don't do dumb things.* Have you ever had something moving along well, and then it gets messed up because you did something dumb? Have you been talking with someone, and all of a sudden something dumb comes out of your mouth? You wonder, "Why did I say that?"

Maybe you make a business decision. You don't wait on God because you think, "It's worked well this far." You just go ahead and do it, and it fails. Don't do dumb things. Walk in wisdom.

Ephesians 5:15-17 in the Amplified Bible reads—
> *Look carefully then how you walk! Live purposefully and worthily and accurately, not as the unwise and witless, but as wise (sensible, intelligent people),*
> *making the very most of the time [buying up each opportunity], because the days are evil.*
> *Therefore do not be vague and thoughtless and foolish, but understanding and firmly grasping what the will of the Lord is.*

We are to walk in wisdom. The New King James Version says,
> *"See then that you walk circumspectly, not as fools but as wise, redeeming the time, because the days are evil.*

Therefore do not be unwise, but understand what the will of the Lord is."

What is wisdom? Wisdom is proper use or application of knowledge. Before you can have knowledge, you must have understanding. If you don't have understanding, it's merely just data or information.

I did pretty well in school, but I had one trouble area, besides conduct: math. Now I could do regular math, but when we got into algebra, let alone calculus, I was lost. I think I missed the first part of pre-algebra or something, because it just didn't click for me.

I tried, and I tried, and I'd go after school to meet with my teacher. I did make some progress. In the early stages of trying to catch up, my teacher said, "You just need to memorize these theorems, and these algorithms." So I went home and memorized them.

Now that was all short-term memory, because I don't have them now. But I memorized these algorithms and theorems. When I walked into class the day of the test, I had studied, but it was just information. It was just raw data, because I didn't understand it. Because I didn't understand, it was not knowledge to me.

I couldn't give proper application of that knowledge, which would be wisdom. Therefore, I blew the test. And so we must have understanding to develop knowledge, in order to walk in wisdom.

Second Peter 1:3 says that as you increase in the knowledge of God, you will have everything you need pertaining to life and godliness. It is through the knowledge of Him. When we get the knowledge of the Word, then we get the knowledge of God, and then we're able to apply that properly. That's wisdom.

Wisdom fosters the conditions for preservation and increase. Isaiah 33:6 says,
> *"Wisdom and knowledge will be the stability of your times, And the strength of salvation; The fear of the Lord is His treasure."*

Wisdom brings steadiness through all seasons. It gives the strength that sustains. Your knowledge of the Lord and your reverence for Him unlock the storehouse.

In Proverbs 8:18, wisdom is speaking.
> *"Riches and honor are with me, Enduring riches and righteousness."*

I don't want something that is not going to last. Did you know that you get what you pay for? Now I am not saying that you've got to get $300 shoes, but if you opt to buy $3 shoes, they'll wear out many times faster than the better ones do.

The things that God gives us don't wear out. We must desire what is enduring.

I want peace that endures. I don't want the peace that the world gives. Did you know that the world does give peace? The peace that the world gives is fleeting. It is actually a false peace. The world only has substitutes for peace. And we only have peace because we had a Substitute.

Wisdom says, *"Riches and honor are with me, Enduring riches and righteousness."* We must walk in wisdom.

When you walk in wisdom, other benefits always accompany it. First Kings 3:5-13 says—

At Gibeon the Lord appeared to Solomon in a dream by night; and God said, "Ask! What shall I give you?"

And Solomon said: "You have shown great mercy to Your servant David my father, because he walked before You in truth, in righteousness, and in uprightness of heart with You; You have continued this great kindness for him, and You have given him a son to sit on his throne, as it is this day.

"Now, O Lord my God, You have made Your servant king instead of my father David, but I am a little child; I do not know how to go out or come in.

"And Your servant is in the midst of Your people whom you have chosen, a great people, too numerous to be numbered or counted.

"Therefore give to Your servant an understanding heart (which is literally wisdom) to judge Your people, that I may discern between good and evil. For who is able to judge this great people of Yours?"

The speech pleased the Lord, that Solomon had asked this thing.

Then God said to him: "Because you have asked this thing, and have not asked for long life for yourself, nor have asked riches for yourself, nor have asked the life of your enemies, but have asked for yourself understanding to discern justice,

"Behold, I have done according to your words: see, I have given you a wise and understanding heart, so that there has not been anyone like you before you, nor shall anyone like you arise after you.

"And I have also given you what you have not asked, both riches and honor, so that there shall not be anyone like you among the kings all your days."

Too often people look at the "things," and they go after the things instead of going after the wisdom. You must walk in wisdom. Never forget that the goal, the focus is wisdom: the wisdom God gives you to make decisions according to His will and purpose.

Colossians 1:9-11 is a prayer I pray every day.

For this reason we also, since the day we heard it, do not cease to pray for you, and to ask that you be filled with the knowledge of His will in all wisdom and spiritual understanding;

that you may walk worthy of the Lord, fully pleasing Him, being fruitful in every good work and increasing in the knowledge of God:

strengthened with all might, according to His glorious power, for all patience and longsuffering, with joy.

Now what do we have here? We ask that we would be filled. You need to pray that for yourself. "Lord, fill me with the knowledge of Your will, in all wisdom and understanding." We need that wisdom. Look at the results of that wisdom. It says that you will be fully pleasing Him, that you would be fruitful in every good work and increasing in the knowledge of God.

Look at this cycle of increasing in the knowledge of God. What follows knowledge then is understanding. We've already asked that we be filled with the knowledge of His will in all wisdom and understanding. You are setting it up to continue to walk in wisdom.

The phrase, "being fruitful in every good work," is a continuous and repeated action. *Always* being fruitful in every good work.

We must walk in wisdom. We cannot walk in our own ideas, saying, "Well, I think this is the way to do it."

"Lean not on your own understanding; In all your ways acknowledge Him, and He shall direct your paths" (Proverbs 3:5, 6). Literally, it will make your paths straight and make them smooth.

We must walk in wisdom. We've got to stop doing dumb things, by taking the time to get the knowledge of God, through knowledge of His Word. We must move over into the realm of understanding and applying it. As you apply that knowledge, you're setting yourself up for preservation and increase.

Wisdom affects everything. It affects your marriage, it affects your children, it affects your health, it affects your finances, your business, it affects relationships. Proverbs 4:7 declares, *"Wisdom is the principal thing; therefore get wisdom."* Wisdom is the principal thing; therefore get wisdom!

The keys are that you *be thankful,* the second key is that you *listen*, and that is to give attention and obedience, the third key is to *walk in wisdom* resulting in obedience. These things must be on your spiritual key ring.

You must live life this way. This is not an on-again, off-again thing. This is a daily walk if you want preservation and increase in your life.

Don't forget that you aren't here just for you, and God's blessings aren't just for you. Yes, He wants to bless you. It gives Him great pleasure to bless you. But ultimately it is for somebody else.

I would hate to think that because I didn't walk in wisdom or wasn't grateful or didn't listen, I messed up where God wanted to use me to help somebody else. I would hate to think that what prevented me was that I did not *preserve* and I did not *increase* what God had brought into my life.

Remember that wisdom is the stability of our times. For these days that we live in, we must have stability. There is nothing out there that is stable. Nothing. Not a thing. But the Word of God is stable. That will be one of the major ingredients in the great outpouring of the Spirit and this great ingathering of the harvest: the stability seen upon the sons and daughters of God.

Walk in wisdom.

6
Shut the Door

The fourth key to playing for keeps is *no openings*. Ephesians 4:27 reads,
   "Nor give place to the devil."

The Amplified Bible says, *"Leave no [such] room or foothold for the devil [give no opportunity to him]."*

The New English Bible says,
   "Leave no loop-hole for the devil."

The enemy looks for every chance to take advantage of us. It is like the story of "Little pig, little pig, let me in." The devil says in such a beguiling way, "Oh, please, just let me in. I only need to rest for a minute."

You don't open the door for the devil! You don't give him place. You don't give him a loophole. You shouldn't even look through the little eye-hole in the door.

He rings the doorbell and says, "I'll give you something nice, if you let me in. Just let me in. I'm not going to hurt you." The devil's a liar. He'll tell you he just wants to visit; he'll just sit on your furniture for a little while. But he'll poke holes in it and everything else. No openings! He comes to steal, to kill, and to destroy.

Let's discuss *sin* for a minute. It's gotten changed lately to "weakness," "indiscretion," or "mistake," but it is still sin. Ask God about it. It's still sin. Sin—disobedience, compromise, or breaking a natural or a spiritual law—is how you give an opening to the devil.

If I get sick, it's because I have broken either a natural or a spiritual law or it is an attack. As a child of God, health is mine. But I have to walk in the commandments and the statutes. I have to follow after God. I have to stay under His covering.

In "God's yard" there are no *sandspurs*. If you come home complaining about *sandspurs*, it's because you've been off in a field. You've got to stay in God's yard.

You sit up late and watch garbage TV. You see a pizza commercial that looks really good. So you call a place to deliver a pizza with everything on it and a two-liter bottle of soda. Now you reason, "You know, this will go flat if I don't drink it tonight." It's about 2:30 a.m. when you finish all of this, and then you've got to get up early.

The next morning you feel like somebody ran you over, and you say, "Oh, the devil is attacking me." No, it wasn't the devil. *You* attacked you.

How do you think you got sick? You broke natural laws. We've got to be careful that we are not overstepping these bounds.

You can also break spiritual laws. What if you need to forgive, and you don't? Did you know it will start to gnaw at you?

What about worrying? Did you know that there is an actual command to cast your cares upon the Lord? It's in First Peter 5:7.

You are not made to carry your cares. If you have a little Yugo automobile, and you are trying to pull a fully loaded semitrailer, it won't work. That car isn't made to handle that. The same is true with you. You're not made to handle it. God says, "Cast all your cares upon Me, and I'll do the caring for you, because I care for you." That's literally what it is saying there.

First Peter 5:7 in the Amplified Bible says,
   "Casting the whole of your care [all your anxieties, all your worries, all your concerns, once and for all] on Him, for He cares for you affectionately and cares about you watchfully."

But what do we do? We just hold on to our burden, and we try to bear it alone. After a while, something is going to burn up. You are not made to handle that. And then you wonder what happened. Why did the Yugo blow up? Because you were trying to use it in a way that it wasn't designed for.

There are sins of omission, and there are sins of commission. You can't compromise, you can't break natural laws, and you can't break spiritual laws. If you break any kind of law, it can have a physical effect upon you, and it can have an emotional effect upon you.

I'm not talking about just going into the grocery store with no shirt and no shoes. Maybe you tried to paint your house when it was 30 degrees out and raining. Then you wonder why you're sick. That goes back to wisdom: don't do dumb things.

"Oh, that devil, he's just after me." No, he's not. He doesn't even have to mess with you. He can watch you bring it on yourself. James 4:17 says,

> *"To him who knows to do good and does not do it, to him it is sin."*

Now we are talking about "No openings." Why no openings? Because we want preservation, and we want increase.

Proverbs 28:13, 18 says—

> *He who covers his sins will not prosper, But whoever confesses and forsakes them will have mercy.*
> *. . . Whoever walks blamelessly will be saved, but he who is perverse in his ways will fall suddenly.*

So really it comes back to us. The choice is ours: to give no opening and to walk in preservation and increase, or to give opening and to allow destruction into our lives.

What is sin? Sin is whatever pulls *you* away from God. If the TV pulls you away from God, that's sin. If your boat pulls you away from God, that's sin. If hunting pulls you away from God, that's sin. If a relationship pulls you away from God, that's sin. It's anything that pulls you away from God. We must understand that sin is the opening that can result in a sudden fall.

Sin will always do this. No matter how harmless it seems, no matter who else is doing it, no matter how great it looks, no matter how good it feels, no matter how secret it is, get ready for this: *sin is meant for your destruction.*

Sin always takes you farther than you want to go, keeps you longer than you want to stay, and costs you more than you want to spend. Sin is meant for your destruction.

It has helped me out about a "bizillion" times to understand that all the devil wants is one shot at me. He says, "Don't just stand there. Come on over into my yard. Just come on over, and it'll be fun!" He just wants one shot. Don't ever forget that. Even if you think you can get away with something, it's meant for your destruction. It's a scheme to destroy you.

James 1:14, 15 says, *"But each one is tempted when he is drawn away by…"* The devil? Oh, I'm sorry.

"But each one is tempted when he is drawn away by his own desires and enticed. Then, when desire has conceived, it gives birth to sin; and sin, when it is full-grown, brings forth death."

Notice here that it says each one is tempted when he is drawn away. One translation says "taken in tow"; another says "dragged away." When you start playing with sin, it is as if you are just hooking up a trailer hitch to your life. It is as if you are cooperating in being pulled away.

Do you know what the result of sin is? Sin takes you away from where you should be. God wants you in the posture of victory, and he wants you in the posture of confidence. But sin immediately undermines your confidence. Then you are quick to give away your victory.

Hebrews 5:12-14 says,
> *For though by this time you ought to be teachers, you need someone to teach you again the first principles of the*

oracles of God; and you have come to need milk and not solid food.

For everyone who partakes only of milk is unskilled in the word of righteousness, for he is a babe.

But solid food belongs to those who are of full age, that is those who by reason of use have their senses exercised to discern both good and evil.

It says that by now you ought to be teaching others. But you don't even have what you had gained previously. Someone must take you back to "square one" again. Sin takes you away from where you should be.

Christianity is not a plateau experience. It is a *glory-to-glory* experience. It is not a roller- coaster experience. It's a glory-to-glory experience. We are not just to get to a point and say, "This is good enough." No, we've got to keep going. Some people know only the verses they knew five years ago. Now, they might be good verses, but we've got to grow.

Some people can't even hold their own. They're a mess, and by this time they should have been teaching and helping somebody else. Do you know what that is? It's sin.

If I know to get into the Word and to grow in the Word, and I don't, that is sin. If I forsake the law of my God, that is sin. If I don't commune and have fellowship with my Creator, that's sin. I've got to press on.

It is sin that keeps us from going where God wants us to go. It is sin that would keep us from being where God wants us to be. We're talking about preservation and increase. The point here is not to let destruction start. *No opening.* No compromise. No negotiation. No détente with the devil.

You don't even need to talk to Satan. Everything he says is a lie. The extent of your conversation with the devil should be to remind him, "You're defeated." You don't need to negotiate. You don't have to haggle it out with him. There is nothing to talk about or explain.

Before every service, I declare the lordship of Jesus and the victory by His blood over our church and over the people. I declare that, and I address the devil personally on the authority of the blood of Jesus. I tell him he has nothing on me, nothing over me, nothing in common with me, nothing to do my ministry or with these services.

And I don't wait for a response. I just declare. "Posted, no trespassing. Cross the line and you're done for, devil!"

No opening. Now the problem is not just the act of sin, but it is the opening that act of sin always creates. That opening brings defilement. *Defile* means to make unfit for blessing, to pollute, or to ruin. Defilement also brings a curse, and it brings destruction.

Imagine that a horrendous sandstorm is blowing outside your house. You decide that you want to go get the newspaper that's on the porch. The wind is so strong that the little prairie dogs are holding onto the cactus. It's blowing! But you've made up your mind to get that paper.

It's just a single act. But what happens? You have to open the door and go out just far enough to pick up your paper. By the time you're back inside, your house has sand, tumbleweeds, and desert critters everywhere. The picture of Grandma over the fireplace has been sandblasted. What happened? You only brought in the newspaper. Look at the harm caused by the opening that single act created.

The King James Version says in Ecclesiastes 10:8,
"Whoso breaketh an hedge, a serpent shall bite him."

You don't create an opening in the wall that surrounds you and keeps you safe. You must stay in God's yard. There are no snakes in God's yard. If you get bitten, it's because you broke the hedge.

Look at the seventh chapter of Joshua, beginning at the first verse, for the destruction a sin can cause.

But the children of Israel committed a trespass regarding the accursed things, for Achan the son of Carmi, the son of Zabdi, the son of Zerah, of the tribe of Judah, took of the accursed things; so the anger of the Lord burned against the children of Israel.

As we follow this through, we find that *one* man committed *one* act of sin, but it created an opening for defilement, destruction, and curse to come against his family and the whole nation. What happened here?

The children of Israel had been strong because of the promises of God and because of His presence. They were assured of victory, and they could walk in confidence and boldness, depending on their God. There was no reason to experience any kind of defeat.

Then they came up against the nation of Ai. They spied it out to see what it would take to win. They decided to send in the "second string" to knock off such an easy opponent.

In the battle, however, the first two or three thousand warriors were failing, and 36 men died immediately. Joshua 7:5 says that the people's hearts melted.

Their courage and strength of purpose just dissolved. Have you had news come suddenly, and your heart melted? These confident, victorious children, the nation of God, walking until now in victory and blessings, were suddenly embarrassed and defeated.

Joshua tore his clothes in distress and fell face-down before God. He said, "Lord, what happened? I guess we would have been better off if we had just stayed on the other side of the Jordan, and lived in our little religious box."

God told Joshua, "Get up. There is sin in the camp." He then instructed him, "In the morning, go from tribe to family to individual, until we get down to the man. I'm going to show you who committed this accursed thing."

Achan was the one who blew it. What he had done was to take a Babylonian garment. Now, where is he going to wear it? It's a forbidden, pagan thing. Is he going to close his tent curtain tight and parade around in his Babylonian garment and then wad it up and hide it again? What could he do with the wedge of silver and fifty shekels of gold he also stole? Others would say, "Achan, where did you get this money?"

I worked in a gas station when I was in high school. The 11-year-old son of the boss would come every other Saturday. His job for the day would be to restock the drink machine and the vending machines. Then he was to take the coins out of the machines and roll them.

He would be in the office for hours, packaging those quarters, dimes, and nickels. When he came out, I'd be leaning on the gas pump or working on something. His pockets would just bulge and jingle. "Hey, Tim, what are you doing?" he'd say. "Want me to buy you a cold drink?"

I'd ask Mr. Moneybags, "Where'd you get all that money?"

"Oh, I've had it," was his answer.

I'd think, "Yeah, for about a half hour."

Achan was in that same kind of spot. Joshua went tribe by tribe. He got down to the family and ran down the family line. God was showing him, and finally he got to Achan. (Verse 19.)

> *Now Joshua said to Achan, "My son, I beg you, give glory to the Lord God of Israel, and make confession to Him, and tell me now what you have done; do not hide it from me."*

If I were Achan, when they announced that they were going to find out in the morning who messed up, I would have found a dumpster in a hurry. But now he was discovered, and he made his confession. (Verses 21, 22.)

> *"When I saw among the spoils a beautiful Babylonian garment, two hundred shekels of silver, and a wedge of gold weighing fifty shekels, I coveted them and took them. And there they are, hidden in the earth in the midst of my tent, with the silver under it."*

> *So Joshua sent messengers, and they ran to the tent;*
> *and there it was, hidden in his tent, with the silver under it.*

The messengers brought the stolen things from the tent, and they brought before the people his sons, his daughters, his oxen, his donkeys, and everything else that was his. The outcome of his act is described in verses 25 and 26.

> *And Joshua said, "Why have you troubled us? The Lord will trouble you this day." So all Israel stoned him with stones; and they burned them with fire after they had stoned them with stones.*
>
> *Then they raised over him a great heap of stones, still there to this day. So the Lord turned from the fierceness of His anger. Therefore the name of that place has been called the Valley of Achor to this day.*

Look what happened here. Joshua said *"Why have you troubled us?"* The whole nation had suffered because of Achan's covetousness. You see, it is not just the act of sin, it's the opening that the act of sin creates that brings all kinds of defilement.

You too may need to find the dumpster. You might have something in your life that is so secret, but it is ruining your business. Or there's suddenly defilement and curse in your family, there are problems, and you can't get along. You had better look at it. And you had better find the dumpster.

First Corinthians 11:31 says,

> *"For if we would judge ourselves, we would not be judged."*

Sin cannot be concealed or contained. It has an acidic quality that cuts through anything. It eventually will show up. I don't care who you are or how smart you are. Be sure of this: your sins will find you out, unless you get rid of them. Find the dumpster, and slam the lid.

I'm glad that we live under the New Testament and that the Holy Spirit will speak to your heart even right now. You can say, "Oh, God, let me just slam-dunk this thing in the spiritual dumpster. Cover me by the blood of Jesus, and push that great big reset button in a hurry, please, God! With Your help, with Your strength, I will serve You, I will obey You, I'll stay straight. Help me, God, help me!" But *you* have to slam that door shut!

Psalm 84:11 says—

For the Lord God is a sun and shield; The Lord will give grace and glory; No good thing will He withhold From those who walk uprightly.

If you want preservation and increase, you've got to walk uprightly before God. You've got to keep the door closed. The only time you ever open the door is when you reach the point of being strong and confident, because you know who you are and how to walk in the authority of God. Then when the devil comes rattling around on your porch, you can open the door and knock him over. Then you can walk him right off your property.

But you never say, "Well, O.K., come in, but just for a minute." Remember, he'll stay much longer than you want him to. And it's going to cost you. It's all up to you.

Did you know that preservation and increase are all up to you? Job 36:11, 12 reads—

If they obey and serve Him, They shall spend their days in prosperity, and their years in pleasures.

*But if they do not obey, They shall perish by the sword,
And they shall die without knowledge.*

Wouldn't you like to spend your days and years in both prosperity and pleasure? It's your choice. Don't give the devil an opening.

Ephesians 5:3 says about sin, *"Let it not be named once among you, as is fitting for saints."* No openings. It is not just that single act of sin. It's the opening, the defilement, the destruction, the curse that comes in as a result. Keep the door closed!

7
Single Minded

B *e single-minded.* James 1:5-8 is a "for instance" scripture. It is setting out a pattern, a way of doing things, that will work if you follow it. The example it uses is wisdom. Verse five reads: *"If any of you lacks"*—for instance—*"wisdom,…"* This principle will work for anything, but James is using wisdom to fill the blank here.

If any of you lacks wisdom, let him ask of God, who gives to all liberally and without reproach, and it will be given to him.

But let him ask in faith, with no doubting, for he who doubts is like a wave of the sea driven and tossed by the wind.

For let not that man suppose that he will receive anything from the Lord;

he is a double-minded man, unstable in all his ways.

The Amplified Bible says in verse eight,

[For being as he is] a man of two minds, (hesitating, dubious, irresolute), [he is] unstable and unreliable and uncertain about everything [he thinks, feels, decides].

If you can't decide between doubt and faith, you are swaying back and forth between two mind-sets. The Bible says not to think for a second you are going to receive from the Lord.

I want to take it a bit further. If you're double-minded, don't think for a second you will be able to *keep* what you've already received. What you receive by faith, you must keep by faith. If you've gained victory in an area of your life by faith, you must keep that victory by faith. If you've gained healing from God by faith, you keep that healing by faith.

If God has blessed your faith, how are you going to keep it? By faith, you continue in it. It's *from faith to faith.* You've got to stay in faith. You need to keep the switch of faith turned on. *Faith works every time, if you leave it on the job.*

Spiritual forces set in motion—and left in motion—have an impact of incredible magnitude. Their power is awesome.

In Matthew 14, Peter is walking on the water. Have you ever walked on water? We used to try to, at youth camp. Peter walked on water, and then he began to sink. When Jesus rescued him, He asked, ***"Oh you of little faith, why did you doubt?"*** (Matthew 14:31).

The word for *little faith* in Greek means "puny, brief, and short duration of belief." What He was saying is this, "Why didn't your faith last?"

It wasn't that Peter didn't have faith. He had faith to step out of the boat, but he didn't keep the "switch of faith" on. He only let his faith stay engaged for a little while. We need to keep the switch of faith turned on.

Then Jesus said, "Why did you doubt?" That word for *doubt* means "being double." In essence, He is saying, "Why did you become double-minded? Why did you give it a second guess? Why did you hesitate?"

Now you should never hesitate when you are on water. If you are water-skiing, and you get something in your eye, you don't say "Hey, slow down a minute!" You don't hesitate on water. And you don't hesitate in life. If God has said something, don't give it another thought. You don't have to second-guess it.

Get fully persuaded and get single-minded. Get your mind made up that "God said it, and that's it." And you stay with that. You've got to get fully assured that preservation and increase are the plan of God. Because if you don't, the devil will talk you out of it.

Isaiah 26:3 is a powerful verse that is for us. It reads,
"You will keep him in perfect peace, Whose mind is stayed on You, Because he trusts in You."

If there is a choice between peace and perfect peace, which one do you want? Perfect peace, of course—peace that is complete and flawless.

That kind of peace comes from fixing your thoughts on the One you can depend on. If God's Word said it, you trust it. Even if the circumstances look contrary, you trust it. You are single-minded. You know how it looks, but you know what God said, and that's what you trust. That's all you need.

Let's reverse the order of the phrases in this verse. "Because he trusts in You, he keeps his mind stayed on You, and because he keeps his mind stayed on You, You keep him in perfect peace." That is the result of being single-minded.

If you are in perfect peace, are you in fear of losing everything you have? No. If you are in perfect peace, are you in fear of what the devil is going to try to put on you? No.

So look at this again. Read it forward and then backward, verse and reverse. "You will keep him in perfect peace whose mind is stayed on You, because he trusts in You." And then, "Because he trusts in You, he keeps his mind stayed on You, and You keep him in perfect peace." What is that? *Single-minded.*

8
Seedtime and Harvest

The sixth key is *sowing*.

Galatians 6:7 says, ***"Do not be deceived, God is not mocked; for whatever a man sows, that he will also reap."***

This is a universal principle that works in every realm. It is called "sowing and reaping."

Verses eight and nine say,

For he who sows to his flesh will of the flesh reap corruption, but he who sows to the Spirit will of the Spirit reap everlasting life. And let us not grow weary while doing good, for in due season we shall reap if we do not lose heart.

The law is this: you plant, you reap. If you sow, you'll eventually have a harvest. I know in the natural that if I go to my backyard and plant corn, I will not grow tomatoes. *What* you sow is *what* you reap.

In Genesis 1:12, we find that God created plants and trees to yield seeds. Each one yields a seed, and that seed produces after its own kind. He established that every seed contains DNA. Basically, that means that the seed is programmed to know what to produce. You don't put it in the ground, and it just becomes whatever it feels like. It is already designated to become a particular thing.

So seed produces after its own kind. John 3:16 declares, **"For God so loved the world that He gave His only begotten Son."**

What did God do? He "sowed" His Son. And what did He reap? Many sons.

That is the wonderful thing about sowing. A farmer plants a kernel of corn, and the stalk grows up. That stalk produces many ears of corn. On each of those ears there are at least 1,000 kernels, and every one of them contains the potential to do the same thing that the original kernel did. Seed produces after its own kind.

Now, McDonald's has this down pat. McDonald's has a Play Land, a clown, and all these talking cookies and dancing French fries. And they have Happy Meals. Have you ever invested in a Happy Meal? Most of us have, especially if you have children.

Notice that Galatians 6:8 says that a man sows to the flesh, or he sows to the Spirit. It's not only what you sow, but what you sow *to*. McDonald's is sowing to children.

I can ask my children, "Anywhere you want to eat?"

"McDonald's" is their answer. And so, children bring parents, and parents bring money. Aha! The clown got you. How? Sowing and reaping. McDonald's has sown. They've done these little extra things, and kids just love it. What you sow, you will reap, and what you sow to, you will reap from.

Look again at verse eight.

"For he who sows to his flesh will of the flesh reap corruption, but he who sows to the Spirit will of the Spirit reap everlasting life."

I'm really glad God didn't get our orders mixed up. You are not sowing to the Spirit and then reaping from the flesh.

Now, it says, "sows to his flesh," which means indulging in the passions and appetites of the flesh. If you just do what your body wants to do, if you indulge in the passions and appetites of your flesh, you are sowing to the flesh, and you will of the flesh reap corruption.

In the Greek, *corruption* means "decay and ruin." You don't want decay and ruin. An understanding of sowing and reaping will help us to be more harvest-oriented, and that will help us to be careful of what we are sowing.

It says, "he who sows to the Spirit"—the capital S shows it is the Holy Spirit. That means being yielded to the guidance and control of the Spirit, instead of the flesh. That is how you sow to the Spirit. The Scripture says that you shall of the Spirit reap everlasting life. You reap everlasting life, which carries with it abundant life.

Then in Romans 8:5, 6 we read,

For those who live according to the flesh set their minds on the things of the flesh, but those who live according to the Spirit, the things of the Spirit. For to be carnally minded is death, but to be spiritually minded is life and peace.

You can see that if you live in agreement with what the flesh wants, you're planting seeds of decay and ruin. But when your actions and your mind are turned toward the Spirit, spiritual seeds are going to grow.

To be *carnally minded* means to be "fleshly minded," so what will the harvest be? It will be death, when it could have been everlasting life and peace.

Your preservation and increase are a result of your sowing. In the Phillips translation, verse seven says this: ***"A man's harvest in life will depend entirely on what he sows."*** The harvest that you are walking in right now is the outcome of the sowing that has already occurred in your life. You might as well admit it. It will set you free to admit it.

First John 1:8 says that if you say you have no sin, the truth is not in you, and you are a liar. That just locks you up. What does the truth do? The truth sets you free. It is best just to say, "Yes, I spilled it. Yes, I broke it."

The fact remains, the sowing you did in the past generated the harvest that you have in life right now. Most people don't want to face that. We want to blame somebody else.

Genesis 8:22 declares,
   "While the earth remains, Seedtime and harvest, cold and heat, winter and summer, And day and night shall not cease."

It is still going on. The earth still remains, and so there is still Seedtime and harvest.

Now understand that harvest is not "if," harvest is "when." If you sow, you will reap. That is the law. It works in every realm, it works in every relationship, it works for people who don't even know God, that if you sow you are going to reap. That is not an "if" situation. You are putting it in the ground, and it is going to come up. It's going to come up in greater force than it went down. So we must understand that our harvest is sure and be very purposeful in our sowing.

We would like a continual harvest of good in our life. The way to ensure a continual harvest is continual sowing. That could be in your finances, that could be in your walk with God. Think about it. You can't take two days to spend with God and expect the whole year to contain the harvest of the presence of God. That won't happen. It is a continual sowing into the Spirit and walking in the things of God.

You can't love and honor your wife or your husband for only one day and say, "That should do it for the week." You need to honor and love your husband or wife, not just one day a week, and not just one month out of the year. We need to be sowing constantly. If you want continual harvest, you need to have continual sowing.

It's the same way in giving. Just because you gave God 10 bucks last year, don't expect that harvest to take you until Jesus comes. You need to continue in the things of God. Continue in sowing.

In Acts 20:35 we read, *"It is more blessed to give than to receive."* Luke, the author, was quoting Jesus, but you can't find it in the gospels. Did Luke make it up? No, I believe this is what happened. Acts 1:3 tells us that after Jesus was resurrected from the dead, He spent 40 days teaching the disciples concerning the things of the kingdom of God.

I believe that during that time He filled in the details for them. He said "All right, now that you've seen all this come to pass, I've got to explain a few things to you." I believe one He taught them was this: "It is more blessed to give than to receive."

We are talking about *preservation and increase.* It is more blessed to give than to receive. When I was a kid, I certainly didn't think that was the case. It seemed as though it was more blessed to receive.

But if you truly understand sowing and reaping, it *is* more blessed to give than to receive. That is because if you are the receiver, that's it. You receive and it's over. When you are the giver, though, what happens? As a giver, you've just started the whole cycle of sowing and reaping. That's why we are blessed to be a blessing: you receive, then you become a giver, and then it continues to cycle through your life.

Now this is important. You must sow seed for the desired harvest. Maybe you're thinking, "I've got some bad harvest. I've sown some bad seed." Well, we'll find out what to do with that.

First, remember that if you have sown, you will reap. If you go to the seed store, you don't want to invest in the manager's special "Seed Surprise," where they just swept the floor and put it in an envelope to sell to you. You want to go down to the seed rack, where every envelope has a picture. That's the picture of the harvest. There might be six varieties of cucumbers. So you look at the pictures, and you find the seed for the harvest that you desire. It is vital to do this.

Now how do you sow? You sow with your words, and you sow with your thoughts. You sow with your actions. Actually, you sow with the motivation behind your actions. You sow with your giving. It's important that we sow for the harvest that we desire.

Let me give you an example. If I sow to the flesh, I shall of the flesh reap what? Corruption —ruin and decay. I don't want ruin and decay. Have you ever had a heated discussion with your spouse? In that heated discussion, do you want ruin and decay? Of course not! Your flesh thinks, "If you say that one more time, I'll tie your hair in a knot." That's what your flesh wants to do. But you don't want ruin and decay.

If you are in that discussion, what you need to sow is mercy. Sure, you have a quick mind, and you can think up something to attack with. Now, don't do that. You need to sow for the harvest that you are desiring. Your husband or wife might be saying, "Yakkity, yakkity, yak," right in your face, but you need to sow mercy.

"Oh, but I don't feel like doing that." That's your flesh talking.

You have a choice here, between the flesh and the Spirit. But what you sow to and what you sow are going to determine what you get back. What you do is to sow mercy, you sow forgiveness, you sow love, and you sow understanding. You must sow for the harvest that you desire.

We've got to take care of it up front. You need to watch what you're sowing into your checkbook. Some people are speaking death over the whole situation. You need to start sowing for the harvest that you desire. Or you might be saying, "These kids of mine are driving me crazy!" We speak all these things, but you can't sow that way. You need to sow for the harvest that you desire.

Now, what if you have sown bad seed? You are probably walking through that bad harvest now. There is a way you can overcome that. Look at Second Corinthians 5:17.

"If anyone is in Christ, he is a new creation; old things are passed away; behold, all things have become new."

It is talking about your spirit man. We're talking about the whole realm of life, but you have to begin somewhere. When you made Christ your Lord, you were born again in your spirit man, but your body and your soul needed to come into line.

Romans 12:1 says that we have to present our bodies living sacrifices, holy and acceptable to God, which is our reasonable service. The Greek actually says that it is the intelligent thing to do. You present your body by bringing it into subjection, and you don't let it rule you. The next verse tells how this is possible: *by renewing your mind.*

I ministered to a man who got born again, but he had some problems because of the seed that he had sown before. Was he born again? Absolutely. If anybody was born again, I believe this man was. But he had been involved in pornography and all kinds of perverted things. He had filled his mind with these things. He sowed seed for that constantly.

Now he prayed the prayer of faith and the prayer of forgiveness. I believe with all my heart he was forgiven, but he came back and said, "I can't get these things out of my mind. They parade through my mind constantly." It was the harvest from all those seeds planted way back when.

Is this man destined for the rest of his life to have a polluted mind? No! It's possible to overcome this harvest.

There are times of deliverance that are as if God just takes it all out, roots and everything. Praise God for those times. My stepfather used to drink a six-pack of beer before supper—and then after that, who knows how many. He also fought a smoking habit. He tried everything to quit.

But when he gave his heart to the Lord and got born again, he was instantly, totally delivered from alcohol and cigarettes. Totally! These things never pulled on him anymore. As a matter of fact, they irritate him.

I wish that was the case for everybody, and I don't know what the difference is. Sometimes God by His grace and mercy comes in and rips up all that old harvest. But there are times that even though we are born again, even though we are new creatures, we are still walking through that old harvest. What do we do?

First John 4:4 says,
> *"You are of God, little children, and have overcome them, because He who is in you is greater than he who is in the world."*

You need to speak that over yourself. You need to look yourself in the mirror and say, "I'm of God. I'm a man of God. I'm born of God." Instead of saying, "I'm a sorry so-and-so," you need to look in the mirror and declare life over yourself.

Then confirm it with First John 5:4, 5.
> *"For whatever is born of God overcomes the world. And this is the victory that has overcome the world—our*

*faith. **Who is he who overcomes the world, but he who believes that Jesus is the Son of God?"***

Jesus is the author and finisher of faith, and so He's the source of faith. If you believe that Jesus is the Son of God, that's the beginning of faith. And what is the victory that overcomes the world? *Our faith.* What I sow is what I reap.

Now watch this. If you have sown bad seed, and all of us have, you will reap a bad harvest. Seed produces after its own kind. You can't walk around and be hateful to people, and you can't run around and be impatient with people and expect a harvest of love and blessings and lilies.

What you sow is what you are going to reap. If you are constantly distrusting and accusatory, then after a while it will come your way. You will reap all the consequences of paranoia and fear. It will come your way. If you steal, it will be stolen. If seed produces after its own kind, and you are sowing those seeds, then you are going to reap of those seeds.

You might say, "Well, I'm born again now, and I want to serve God, and I'm tired of this old harvest in my life." Then you must sow for the harvest you are desiring. *The seeds of faith overcome the other seeds.* You must constantly, consistently sow seed that counteracts the old harvest and will choke it out at the roots. Eventually it will be out of your life.

That is why the Bible has given you instruction to renew your mind and to cast down imaginations and ***"every high thing that exalts itself against the knowledge of God, bringing every thought into captivity to the obedience of Christ"*** (2 Cor. 10:5).

It is almost as if you are clearing out and reaping out that old harvest, and you are planting in the new seeds of faith. Faith overcomes.

So if you are walking in the old harvest, you need to sow seed. It may take a little while, but you need to sow seed, constantly sow seed. Now by faith, it is going to choke out that old harvest, and there will be a day that you will walk free from that old harvest.

Think about it. You may have run up a lot of debt and bad bills from years before. Are you destined to stay in that forever? No, you can start today changing the whole situation. You start communicating with your creditors, and you start sowing seeds of trust and integrity. You start making an honest effort. You put in a good day's work. You start handling your money more responsibly. You begin to tithe and give offerings. You pay bills. You go on and you sow financial seed. Eventually, that financial burden is going to be so far in the past that it is gone. No more dodging people all the time because "everybody you know, you owe."

You don't have to be walking in that old harvest. Start the new harvest. Sow seeds of what is right. Sow to the Spirit, and you will of the Spirit reap life. This is good news for you today. Sowing is a key to preservation and increase.

9

For Believers Only

The seventh key to preservation and increase is *willingness to be misunderstood.*

In Romans 3:3 we read,

For what if some do not believe? Will their unbelief make the faithfulness of God without effect?

You answer that, "No way!"

If I have received the Word of God into my life, and I have set my faith on receiving something, and someone next to me doesn't believe that way, do I have to back off from what I believe? Not if I have the Word of God on it. I'll stand on the Word. They can stand on whatever they want to, but I'm standing on the Word.

"Well, I just don't believe that way."

"Well, that's you, brother. That's you, sister. I'm standing right here. I'm not going anywhere. Don't try to talk me out of it. My mind is made up. My heart is settled."

Usually your worst opposition is either from family or from religious folks. But the very worst is religious folks that are family. They can even make you hate the holidays.

Hebrews 4:2, 3 says—

For indeed the gospel was preached to us as well as to them; but the word which they heard did not profit them, not being mixed with faith in those who heard it. For we who have believed do enter that rest.

Religious people all have access to a Bible. And they all have access to hearing the Word of God preached. The Word was delivered to them just as it was delivered to us.

What's the difference? They didn't mix faith with the Word that they heard. So what happened? It did not profit them. Instead, in the form of religion, they begin to explain it away, trying to show why it doesn't work for them. Some would rather accuse God and say He stopped doing something than to say that somehow they had missed it.

If you miss your healing, it isn't God's fault. If you missed an answer to prayer or an answer to a situation, it wasn't God's fault. Religion will explain it away: "Oh, that went out with the disciples." No. The problem is these people heard the same Word, but they didn't mix it with faith. So they didn't profit by it.

That tells us that if we will hear the Word and mix it with faith it will profit us. This isn't just talking about money. Money is the least. But it is necessary.

We're talking about *being willing to be misunderstood.* Some people don't know what real prosperity is. You must know what the Bible says and not retreat from it because someone has said something against you.

But most people tend to do that. If somebody criticizes them, they decide, "I just won't say it anymore, because I don't want anybody to call us a prosperity cult." We are not a prosperity cult. We are believers. We are the children of God, and His Word works for us.

Prosperity comes from soul prosperity. Third John 2 says, ***"Beloved, I pray that you may prosper in all things and be in health, just as your soul prospers."***

Some people think that prosperity is some extra money in their pocket. But without soul prosperity, they can't even handle the money they already have. God can't trust you to receive a financial increase if your soul isn't growing and thriving in Him. He wants to see that you won't be confused by it if He blesses you.

Remember, if God can get it through you, God can get it to you. Psalm 35:27 says that He takes pleasure in the prosperity of His servants.

Prosper literally means "to flourish." It means to be all-around healthy, with all your leaves green. That's what God wants in your life: peace of mind, health, and financial confidence. Just because somebody else criticizes that or doesn't understand it, do you think I'm going to abandon it? Forget it. It works!

Some folks, especially religious folks, will fight you to stay sick, to stay broke, and to stay depressed. They say, "Well, bless God, He is teaching me something." There's a better way to learn, brother!

Don't you just love those things that you have to assemble? They lie to you. They say "some" assembly required. You take the

93

little instruction sheet out of the box and lay it aside. Then you dump out all these parts. This is what religious people do. They say, "We're going to learn. We know God will teach us."

Four days later, they've got this thing. They don't know what it is, and they've ruined half the parts. It doesn't fit together, and it looks dumb. You say to them, "What is the problem?"

"God's teaching me something."

There's a better way, friend. Why don't you take the instructions? Mix it with faith, which is corresponding action. Part A goes with Part B. Before you know it, you've got the thing all together, and you're using it.

Some people want to change the "good news" to just "news," or "bad news." They want to take out all the good. If I were lying in a hospital bed, and somebody offered to pray that God would heal me, I'd say, "Hey, I want to hear about this. You mean He heals? Tell me about it." Then, they could share that with me, I'd hear the Word and mix it with faith, and it would profit me. But so many will insist on staying sick, or staying broke, or staying depressed.

This is the truth of redemption: *The devil cannot legally lay on you what God has already laid on His Son.* He laid sickness and disease on Jesus. So the devil can't legally lay that on you. You've got to know your legal rights. Depression is far from me. Oppression is far from me. Why? Because I am redeemed from it.

You have to know that you are redeemed, and you have to be willing to be misunderstood. What if they don't understand? Does that make the faithfulness of God of no effect? Does that mean the promises are no good because somebody else doesn't believe them? As for me, it works for me. It's to him who believes.

Do you believe it? That's the key. Are you fully persuaded? Is your heart, is your mind made up? That's what counts.

Jesus had the most trouble with religious folks. With the prostitutes, the drunkards, and the tax collectors, He had great success. It was the religious folks. They are still in the earth today.

The Pharisees believed the Word. They held fast to the Word. They loved the Word so much that they applied it to their life strenuously. If it said to rest on the Sabbath, they'd say, "Let's measure this out. Don't take more than 30 steps on the Sabbath." So they took the written law, and then they came up with the oral law to go along with it. They came up with all these applications and restrictions. "Don't do this, don't do that, don't do this, don't do that."

The tragedy was that they put the written law and their oral traditions side by side. They held them all with the same esteem. They got so locked into all of it. Now, they loved the Word. They were looking for a Messiah, too.

In Matthew 23:23, Jesus told these people—
> *Woe to you, scribes and Pharisees, hypocrites! For you pay tithe of mint and anise and cummin, and have neglected the weightier matters of the law: justice and mercy and faith. These you ought to have done, without leaving the others undone.*

Picture this. They're in their little gardens. They know that the tithe is holy to the Lord and that they are to give Him the first fruit of all their increase. Since they are so literal in applying the law, they're tithing of their plants of mint, anise, and cummin. They're counting leaves, so that they can find which ones to tithe.

But all the while they're forgetting about justice and mercy and faith, because they are so wrapped up in their own little thing. While somebody over here needs help, somebody over here needs love, they're saying, "Don't bother me, I'm counting leaves. I've got to tithe." They missed the whole point.

We too can be religious. We can love God, and we can go to church. As Norval Hayes says "Bluebirds love God, and rats go to church." You can love God and go to church, but that's not going to get it for you. Focus on doing the things He says are most important.

Then there were the Sadducees. They held to the law and believed it, but they didn't believe in anything supernatural. They didn't believe in resurrection—nothing after life. They didn't like the Pharisees either. They hardly agreed with them on anything.

Jesus told the religious people that their traditions had made the Word of God of no effect. (Mark 7:9-13.) The most powerful thing against the Word of God is tradition. That's why some people get stuck in their tradition and won't hear truth. They will fight you to stay sick, when the Bible says that Jesus bore our sicknesses and carried our diseases. (Matthew 8:17.)

We've got to hold fast to truth and be willing to be misunderstood. It's important to realize that not all religious folks and not all Christian folks are *believers*. I didn't say they wouldn't make it to heaven. I said they are not believers.

When you know what's right, you're willing to be misunderstood. You don't water it down and compromise to the lowest common denominator. You hold fast to the truth.

Romans 1:16 says,
"For I am not ashamed of the gospel of Christ, for it is the power of God to salvation for everyone who believes."

There is a power to salvation. Salvation implies deliverance, safety, preservation, healing, and soundness. You have got to know that salvation is more than just the forgiveness of sins.

Praise God that it *is* the forgiveness of sins. But it is much more than that. If it is just the forgiveness of sins, then all we are going to do is create another mess of sin. It is much more than that. The power of God, the power of the good news of Christ, the Anointed One, is released in those who believe.

Ephesians 1:19 tells us we can know **"... what is the exceeding greatness of His power toward us who believe, according to the working of His mighty power."**

In Mark 16:18, Jesus says signs shall follow those who believe. One of the signs is that they lay hands on the sick, and the sick do recover. Yet some will say, "Well, we don't believe that." Do you know what? Those signs don't follow them.

Are they going to heaven? I think they'll make it, because it didn't say, "If you lay hands on the sick, you'll make it to heaven." It said if you make Jesus Lord, if you make Him Savior, if you call upon the name of the Lord, you will make it to heaven.

But the Bible also says these signs will follow those that are on their way—those that believe. They'll lay hands on the sick, and they'll recover.

Now, I've had people tell me, "Well, I don't believe that."

"Well, then don't lay hands on the sick, because it won't work for you." I happen to believe it, and I happen to do it, and I happen to get people healed. A man with an experience is never at the mercy of a man with an argument. So you've got to be willing to be misunderstood. Don't be ashamed of the truth.

John 8:32 says, *"And you shall know the truth, and the truth shall make you free."* That word *free* in the Greek means "liberated, the result of redemption." I want you to consider this next statement. *Don't forsake truth for acceptance.* Truth frees. Acceptance binds. You don't forsake truth for acceptance.

Recently I ran into a man I had known since I was in high school. I knew him from a denominational church. I hadn't seen him for a long time. He said, "How are you doing?"

I said, "Real good."

He said, "What are you doing up here?"

I said, "Well, I'm pastoring a church up here."

"That's right, I heard that you're a pastor." I shared a few things of how God was blessing. Then he said, "Well, what do you all believe?"

I began to list a few things. He started discounting them. "You don't believe such-and-such, do you, and you don't believe such-and-such, do you?" It was like going into the Word of God and saying,"Yeah, this is a good one. Let's get rid of that. And get rid of that one too."

I said,"Well, let me just tell you what we believe. We believe that a lot of people by their traditions have made the wonderful good news of the Word of no effect. So we just believe the Word of God, and you know what? People are being changed, refreshed, and blessed by that."

"Well, good to see you." And he went on his way. Now, he loves God, and I'll see him in heaven. But he could have had a much better time down here.

Remember this: you must be willing to lose friends and family to gain Jesus, so that you can win friends and family to Jesus. The typical pattern is that you get born again, and your friends say, "Oh, you got religion." Show them you don't have *religion*. Show them you have the life of God in you. You blossom, and it grows and continues to flourish in your life.

You've got to be willing to be misunderstood. Don't forsake truth to get acceptance. People will back away from the truth they have received, because of their friends. If you want to keep them longer, be willing to lose them now to gain Jesus. Then you can really get full of Jesus, so that you win your friends and family back to the Lord. That's the key.

They might not understand you, but you stay in place, and they'll be back. They might mock you right now, but you stay in place and let them see the life of God in and on you. Let them see the blessings of God in you, let them see the love and anointing that will cover your life as you stay put and walk in preservation and increase, and eventually they'll come back.

They'll be the ones picking up the phone and saying sheepishly, "I'm sick. Could you pray for me, or whatever you do?" They'll come around. And do you know what God will do? You'll pray for them, and you'll be able to carry them at that point on your faith, and God will touch them.

Then you can call them up and say, "Hey, what happened?"

"Well, it ran its course."

"No, no, it didn't. Didn't you ask me to pray? I prayed. And when I pray, my Father God answers. He touched you. Do you know why He touched you? Because He loves you. He wants to get past your hard head and show you that He loves you."

Remember we are willing to be misunderstood. We are not *trying* to be misunderstood, but we are *willing* to be. You know most people who misunderstand me have only heard *of* the teacher but have not heard the teacher. Most people who misunderstand you haven't taken the time to sit down with you and let you in the gentleness of the Holy Spirit share what and why you believe. But you can sit there and say, "You know, I used to not have any peace until the Prince of Peace came. I know you may not understand all that, but it is so real in my life." Let God work.

First Corinthians 15:57, 58 says—
> **But thanks be to God, who gives us the victory through our Lord Jesus Christ. Therefore, my beloved brethren, be**

steadfast, immovable, always abounding in the work of the Lord, knowing that your labor is not in vain in the Lord.

Look at that word *immovable*. Do you know what it carries with it? The implication that somebody tried to move it—somebody who found out the Christians couldn't be budged. They were steadfast. And they were always abounding. Why? Because their thanks were to God, who gives us the victory through Jesus.

Does everybody understand me? I don't know. I do care. But I don't know, and it doesn't change what I believe. You just stay there, and if they turn and walk off, they'll be back, if you stay there. You have to be willing to be misunderstood.

Again, don't try to be misunderstood. But be willing to. You just be steadfast, immovable, always abounding in the work of the Lord, knowing that your labor in Him is not in vain.

10
Add to Your Faith

T he eighth key is *adding to your faith.*

Hebrews 11:1 reads,
"Now faith is the substance of things hoped for, the evidence of things not seen."

You must first have hope. The Bible says that those who are without hope are usually those who are without God. (Eph. 2:12.) Never become godless, because if you become godless in your thinking, you also become hopeless.

As long as you have God, as long as you have His Word, you can be filled with hope. Then faith can give substance—reality—to the things that you hope for. If you have a relationship situation, a physical situation, a financial situation, or whatever, you have hopes concerning them. You have hopes for your children. You have goals, you have dreams, and you have hopes. Faith brings substance and reality to these hopes.

Hebrews 11:6 says,
"But without faith it is impossible to please Him, for he who comes to God must believe that He is, and that He is a rewarder of those who diligently seek Him."

Without faith, you cannot please God. You must first believe that He is. If you don't have the faith to believe that He is, then you will never diligently seek Him, and then you will never receive from God. It pleases God to bless us and to see us operate in faith. But without faith, you can't please Him.

First John 5:4 declares, *"...And this is the victory that has overcome the world—our faith."* If anybody tells you, "Come to Jesus, and you won't have any more problems," they are telling you a story. You have a whole new set of problems. Things that never bugged you before bug you now. Things that were no problem at all to do are a problem to do now. You have a new set of standards and a new way of thinking. You've become a new creature. If somebody says that you will have no problems, they are just flat out telling you a lie.

But the good news is this. You can overcome any problem that would come your way. Problems come, but they don't have to overcome.

Jesus said in John 16:33, *"... In the world you will have tribulation;..."* Even though we aren't *of* the world, we are certainly in it. The Amplified Bible says to expect *"tribulation and trials and distress and frustration."* Have you had any of those?

Jesus said, *"... But be of good cheer."* Don't stop right there, though. You have to read the whole verse. *"But be of good cheer, I have overcome the world."* The Amplified Bible adds, *"I have deprived it of power to harm you and have conquered it for you."*

Do I still have the problems? Do I still have the distress, the frustration, the trials, the tribulations? Yes and amen. But I am of good cheer, because He has overcome them for me, and so by my faith in Him and what He has done for me, I too can overcome those things.

Now, by faith we receive, by faith we access the promises of God, and by faith we bring abundant life into our life and into our situation. By faith you receive, by faith you preserve, and by faith you increase. So it is important that we look at faith here. Your faith is very important. Keep this all in the perspective of preservation and increase and "playing for keeps."

The devil is after your faith. What do I mean by faith? I mean your confidence in God and your confidence in God's Word. The devil is after your confidence, so he is after your faith. First Peter 5:8 reads, ***"Be sober, be vigilant; because your adversary the devil..."*** *Adversary* is the Greek word *antidikos*, which means "against a cause." The devil is against you, and he is against your cause for God.

> ***"Be sober, be vigilant; because your adversary the devil walks about like a roaring lion, seeking whom he may devour."***

The word *seeking* here means "plotting against." The devil is a schemer, and he is always devising ways to come against you. He knows what "pulls" on you. How does he know? You keep telling him and showing him.

Let's say you're a monkey in the bush. If I want to get you out of the bush, then I try to see what attracts you. If I put an ugly spider out there, you're not going to reach out for it. But if I roll a jingly ball across there, your little hairy hand might come out. Or if I sprinkle some Raisinettes along there, your little hairy hand comes out. And if I sprinkle them a little farther away, your little hairy hand, shoulder, and head emerge. Here you come, out of the bush.

You see, the devil is trying to get you out of that place of covering and shelter. He knows what pulls on you, so you need to ignore some things. You'll gain greater strength and victory over some things if you walk right past them. Walk right past them and ignore them.

Every time you do that, you get stronger and more victorious over them. If you have some things pulling on you, walk past them. If the refrigerator is pulling on you, just walk on past it.

In the mall, if you see somebody that is very pretty, and you shouldn't be looking, walk right on past—and not just because your wife is with you. I know one brother who actually wrecked his vehicle. He was doing well to just keep his eyes on the road. There are a lot of things that pull on you, and you need to be careful that you don't "show and tell" the devil which ones they are.

He's out to get you, and he is plotting. He says, "Now, how can I get this guy? I know what pulls on him. Let's put this in his path." He's going to draw you out there and get you. It will help you today if you will take hold of this.

Peter says that the devil walks about like a roaring lion, seeking whom he may devour. That word *devour* means to "drink down, to gulp entire." Remember how as a child you'd be out playing in the yard, you'd be all hot and sweaty, and your mom would call you for dinner? There would be a big, cold glass of ice tea, and before she could even get to the table, gulp, gulp, gulp, and it was gone. "Where did that go?"

"I gulped it down."

You see, the devil is seeking people he can gulp right down. On TV back in the '60s, they would actually swallow live goldfish. I never tried it, but maybe you did. That's what the devil wants to do to you: just gulp you down.

There are five kinds of people he has no trouble swallowing up. First are the *wounded.* These are people that get their feelings hurt, and they get their hopes dashed. Think of a flock of sheep. Truly there is safety in numbers by staying with the flock.

It's like my kids sometimes. They'll be fussing, and I'll ask, "What's wrong?"

"He touched my arm."… "She looked at me."

With some people, it doesn't take much to get them wounded. Then they think, "Well, I'm going over here and lick my wounds. I'll just see if anybody cares." There are folks that do that.

Another category is the *wandering.* This is Little Betty Church-Hop. She ends up going from church to church. "Well, they have this wonderful speaker, and they have this, and they have that," or "I'm going to stay home and watch this other preacher on TV." They never get planted. They just wander around.

The devil, roaming about as a roaring lion, says, "I'm going to get that one. The way that one is wandering around, that's going to be some juicy snack." So he is looking for those to gulp down.

The Bible teaches, "no roots, no fruit." (Prov. 12:12.) You must become planted, because if you're not, you're not a part of any sheepfold. If you're off out there wandering, then you are very vulnerable to the devil.

Another category is the *wondering*. We have the *wounded* and the *wandering,* and now we have the *wondering*. They just haven't settled some major issues. First Peter 3:15 says to be always ready to give a reason for the hope that is within you. You need to know what you believe and why you believe it.

Some people say, "Well, I don't know if Jesus is a healer or not." You'd better nail that down. You'd better find out.

"Well, I don't know if He'll give me peace of mind or not. I don't know if He can help me out of this situation or not." You'd better find out! When you have questions, do you know what it is? It's the Holy Spirit trying to lead you into a Bible study. If you have something you're not sure of, track it down. Get in the Word.

The Holy Spirit is trying to get you well rounded. He's guiding you into all truth. You need to get that nailed down in your life. Quit being a wonderer, because the devil comes around and says, "Let's get the guy with the blank look on his face."

Another category is the *weak*. The weak are those who pass up the nourishment they need. They won't eat the meat of the Word, let alone the milk of the Word, so they remain weak. They won't plug into the power source of God by worshiping and praying. They won't gain the strength that comes from the corporate anointing of being with other believers. So they remain weak. Yes, they'll get to heaven, but they remain weak.

You cannot be weak, because the devil sees you tagging along and falling behind the rest of the flock. He'll come along and eat you up.

The last category is the *whining*. When you're whining, you quit looking at the task at hand. You start whining and turning around every way. "Ying, yang, ying yang, ying, yang. Whine, whine, whine, whine."

The devil says, "This will be a cinch." Whiners are easy to pick off.

Whatever category you might fit in, be careful, because the devil is after your faith. He wants to destroy you.

Satan is the god of this world's system. His system is designed to erode your faith. When you just go out into the world and go to your job, nothing wants to build your faith. The newspaper you read and the conversations you hear aren't building your faith. They are designed to erode your faith. Billboards, TV, magazines, and the other media all around you are pulling on you. They are distracting you and trying to wear down your courage and your faith.

Nothing out there will build your faith. That's why you have to be still, that's why you have to withdraw for periods of time, and that's why you have to seek that secret place. (Psalm 91:1.) You have to find that secret place. And do you know what? The devil can't find that secret place, because it's a secret place. The Holy Spirit will show it to you. When you get in that place, you find everything that you need.

Second Peter 1:2, 3 reads—

Grace and peace be multiplied to you in the knowledge of God and of Jesus our Lord,

as His divine power has given to us all things that pertain to life and godliness, through the knowledge of Him who called us by glory and virtue.

The knowledge of Him. It's not knowing about Him. It's knowing *Him*. You can ask just about anybody, and they can tell you something about Him. But it's knowing Him. It's this intimate, personal knowing Him.

As you get acquainted with all the factors and facets of God, you'll have not only grace and peace multiplied to you, but look what else you will have from knowing Him that way. You will have all things that pertain to life and godliness. Natural and spiritual.

Verses 4 and 5 continue—

By which have been given to us exceedingly great and precious promises, that through these you may be partakers of the divine nature, having escaped the corruption that is in the world through lust.

But also for this very reason, giving all diligence, add to your faith...

There is a reason for making very sure to add to your faith. So that you can have grace and peace multiplied to you. So that you can have everything that you need for life and godliness. So that you can have exceedingly great and precious promises, and so that you can escape the depravity and corruption of the world.

How do you add to your faith? You do it with all diligence. What the body of Christ needs these days is a great big injection of diligence. Now, there is nothing wrong with these little bread boxes of scripture promises, but if that's the extent of your devotional life, you're in trouble. You're in big trouble.

I advocate reading a Proverb a day, but if that is all the food you're getting, you're in trouble. There must be a diligence added to this. There can be no more sloppy Christianity. You know, we need to be a little hard on ourselves. We need to judge ourselves.

There are times when you're a little bit sleepy and you know you haven't been in the Word, and you haven't prayed. Why give up *life* to have a little bit of sleep?

You know God will never be a debtor to you. If He wakes you up in the middle of the night to pray, you won't be all worn out in the morning. God is not going to cheat you that way. If you give up something, He'll take care of it. God will never owe you anything. You can never out give God. Even if you give up houses and land, He'll give you back a hundredfold.

We have to apply some diligence. We have to press in. It's time to make up our minds and say, "I'm going to get into the presence of God today. I'm going to make the time. I'm going to dig in the Word today until I get some fresh manna, some revelation from God."

It takes some diligence. Some translations render that word *diligence* as "employ every effort." Another translation says, "make it your whole concern." Yet another one says, "do your level best."

Continuing in 2 Peter 1:5, it says, *"But also for this very reason, giving all diligence, add to your faith..."* Let's look briefly at the things we are to add to our faith.

At this point, you might be wondering what's wrong with your faith. Can't your faith just make it? No, your faith is such a precision instrument that it must have these proper things surrounding it to give it balance, to give it protection, to help fortify it. Your faith is what the devil is after.

You don't need to be using your faith to keep your faith. You need to put your faith into action and use these things that keep you balanced so that you stay on track. What I'm about to share with you, religion will say, can't occur. But I'm going to show it to you out of the pages of the Bible. You can see it work in your life, also!

Verses 5-7 read—
　　... Giving all diligence, add to your faith virtue, to virtue knowledge,
　　　to knowledge self–control, to self–control perseverance, to perseverance godliness,
　　　to godliness brotherly kindness, to brotherly kindness love.

Let's look at these briefly. *Virtue* is moral excellence, integrity, energy. You have to add that to your faith. Then add to that *knowledge.* Knowledge is intelligence with understanding.

Third is *temperance.* Temperance is self–control or restraint. It also includes continence. Continence means abstaining, or quitting. It refers to the appetites of the flesh, chiefly sexual appetites.

If you are involved in any form of sexual sin, be it in your mind or in your life, the only way you are going to walk in victory is to have continence. You must have some restraint. You must have some self–control. You can't keep justifying to yourself why you're involved, or why you are letting yourself think something.

Men of God don't think or act that way. Women of God don't think or act that way. So if you want to walk free of those things, you must use all diligence to add temperance or self–control to your faith.

Next is ***patience.*** Patience is steadfastness, or constancy. It is cheerful and hopeful endurance. Most people think of perseverance or patience as "I'm just hanging in here coping until something happens." No, it's cheerful and hopeful expectation and endurance.

Next is ***godliness***, which means holiness, holy living that imitates God. Holiness in a person's life is not wearing your hair a certain way or dressing a certain way or saying, "I will not do this," or "I will not do that." That's not holiness.

Holiness is a product of the Holy Spirit in your life. What makes a person evil? Evil influences or spirits in his life. So godliness is the beneficial result of the Holy Spirit in our lives.

Add to godliness, ***brotherly kindness.*** Brotherly kindness is affection that is volitional. That means you *will* to do it. It is deliberate, and that means that you do it *on purpose*. It boils down to this: Christian courtesy.

Galatians 6:10 says,

"... Do good to all, especially to those who are of the household of faith."

Do good to all. That is brotherly kindness. It's affection. It's volitional and deliberate. You don't just come to church and go out, saying, "Well, I got blessed." You need to look for somebody there to bless. There are people who come in and go out every week alone. You need to say, "Holy Spirit, point out somebody today that I can show brotherly kindness to."

Next is **love**—agape love. This is a love you extend to a person, but not just because you like them. We all know that it's easy to love somebody that you like. I like my wife, and she is easy to love. People around us need agape love, but we don't extend it, because we think, "I don't like them."

This is important to understand. Agape love is unconditional. It is God's love in you and through you. You extend that love because they need that love, not because you like them. The person that does you wrong—you extend to them agape love. Because you like them or because they deserve it? No, because they need the love that you have. Love never fails. No matter what the situation is, love never fails.

Verse 8 begins, *"For if these things."* What things? Virtue, knowledge, temperance, patience, godliness, brotherly kindness, and love. *"For if these things are yours, and abound, you will be neither barren nor unfruitful in the knowledge of our Lord Jesus Christ."*

We have come full circle here. If you will add these seven things to your faith, so that they abound — increase and overflow

— you will neither be barren nor unfruitful in the knowledge of our Lord Jesus Christ.

Through the knowledge of Him, you have grace and peace multiplied to you (verse 2). You have everything that you need for life and godliness (verse 3). You have exceedingly great and precious promises, and you escape the corruption that is in this world through lust (verse 4). All of that comes by adding those things to your faith.

Notice verse 9.
> *"For he who lacks these things is short sighted, even to blindness, and has forgotten that he was cleansed from his old sins."*

If you *don't* add these things to your faith, you'll lose your way, and you'll forget that you are even redeemed. You'll come back under the condemnation and curse of the devil. Instead of walking in the light, you'll only grope your way through life. I didn't say you wouldn't make it to heaven, but you're not going to look like much when you get there.

Verse 10 says,
> *"Therefore, brethren, be even more diligent to make your call and election sure, for if you do these things you will never stumble."*

Peter has already told us to give all diligence. Now he sees this again right in front of him, and he says to be all the more diligent to keep these qualities of character guarding your walk of faith.

Nobody likes to stumble. It says to be even more diligent, keep on doing these things, and you will never stumble. *Stumble* means "to fall or to be tripped up."

Look down in verse 11.

"For so an entrance will be supplied to you abundantly into the everlasting kingdom of our Lord and Savior Jesus Christ."

"Everlasting" there again points out preservation and increase. The entrance that is supplied to you in the kingdom of God is not just heaven. You won't need grace in heaven, you won't need peace, you won't need promises. You won't need anything pertaining to life or to godliness.

In heaven you won't have to worry about the corruption that is in the world, and you won't have to worry about falling. When do you need grace, peace, and God's promises? *You need them now!*

You won't need them in heaven, because heaven is perfect—because heaven is God. The Bible says in Revelation 21:27, **"But there shall by no means enter it anything that defiles."** In heaven nothing gets "messed up." Heaven is wonderful.

I can't wait to see heaven, but I'm going to keep busy until I get there. Jesus says, "Occupy, do business until I come, get busy, make the most of every opportunity, press on, walk in wisdom, and be diligent." (Luke 19:13.) When He comes again, He'll find you doing! Abundant life is what He came to give. You can enjoy that now and forever.

Remember that we are talking about preservation and increase. We are talking about the things that come in our lives. How did you receive anything from God? By His grace and His mercy, of course, but how do you access that? Through faith.

It is so important now that we give all diligence to add to our faith. In adding to our faith, then we will be fruitful and abounding in the knowledge of Him.

As we are fruitful and abounding in the knowledge of Him, grace and peace are multiplied, everything that we need for life and godliness, the great and exceedingly precious promises are ours, and we will not stumble. And we will have an abundant entrance into abundant life.

That's really good news.

11

Fear Not!

B *e fearless.* Matthew 28:1-4 says—

> *Now after the Sabbath, as the first day of the week began to dawn, Mary Magdalene and the other Mary came to see the tomb.*
>
> *And behold, there was a great earthquake; for an angel of the Lord descended from heaven, and came and rolled back the stone from the door, and sat on it.*
>
> *His countenance was like lightning, and his clothing as white as snow.*
>
> *And the guards shook for fear of him, and became like dead men.*

If any guard under the Roman authority did not fulfill a task, he was killed. Aren't you glad you don't work for that company?

Remember the Philippian jailer? When the earthquake came, Paul and Silas got an early release from prison. Then the jailer drew his sword to kill himself. Paul said, "Do yourself no harm."

So these guards in Jerusalem took their jobs seriously and for a good reason. Now think about their assignment. When guards were appointed to a task like this, they went in groups of four, but this one didn't seem like much of a responsibility. There was a big rock in front of a tomb, and they just had to make sure that the dead man stayed in the tomb. That shouldn't have been any problem.

They also had to make sure those Christians didn't come around and try to manipulate the facts. This tomb had been sealed by a cord across the opening, over the stone. Each end of the cord had a clay seal with an emblem on it, to show if there had been any tampering.

The four guards were standing there, when the ground began to shake violently. Then here came an angel out of heaven, a creature of dazzling brightness.

I don't think they tried to stop him. He probably just walked past them with a big grin and rolled the stone away. Then he climbed up on the stone and sat on it.

The guards were overwhelmed. One translation says, "They fell over like corpses." These guards were very strong, very skilled, highly trained, and well equipped. But fear did something to them. Fear paralyzed them and completely neutralized them.

Fear can paralyze you. There are people that are prisoners in their homes because of fear. There are people who just won't step out and do things because of fear. There are people who won't make decisions because of fear.

A man went to his pastor and said, "Pastor, I've been in this job for ten years. I've gone as far as I can go with the company. I would like for you to agree with me in prayer that I could get a job doing such and such, and that I could advance. I really know I would enjoy doing this other thing." The pastor agreed in prayer with him.

About two months later, an opportunity opened up for him. He came back to the pastor and said, "Pastor, I have a problem."

He said, "What's the problem?"

"Well, there is an opening here in this company for the very job that I want."

"Praise God!" the pastor said.

"No, no. You don't understand. What if I step out, and it doesn't work? What if I get over there and I don't like it? And what if, what if, what if?"

Now because of fear, do you know what he did? He didn't take the job. He stayed right where he was. Fear can paralyze you. Fear can keep you in the same old place. Some people are unwilling to do anything because of their fear. We have to become fearless.

Chapter 9 of the Book of John shows how fear can cause you to miss out. John 9:1 says,

>*"Now as Jesus passed by, He saw a man who was blind from birth."*

He had been blind all his life. That's a long time. So the disciples asked a question. This question used to bother me, and Jesus' response used to bother me, until I looked a little further at it. They said, "Lord, who sinned—this man or his parents? Who sinned?"

Jesus said, "Nobody sinned. This isn't because of sin. It's so that the works of God would be revealed." The King James Version says, "should be made manifest in him."

What is this? Did God create somebody wrong so that He could fix him in public? First of all, that doesn't fall into the character and the nature of God. Second, you have to understand about affliction, sickness, and disease. Those things come from the devil.

Remember Acts 10:38:
"How God anointed Jesus of Nazareth with the Holy Ghost and with power, who went about doing good and healing all who were oppressed by the devil, for God was with Him."

Remember the woman who was bent over, in Luke 13:11-17. Jesus said in verse 16,
"... Ought not this woman, being a daughter of Abraham, whom Satan has bound—think of it—for eighteen years, be loosed from this bond...?"

He is calling her a daughter of God's covenant to bless Abraham. He blames her problem on a spirit of affliction from Satan.

We know that Jesus carried away our sickness and our disease. He's done away with those things. So it doesn't fit God's "MO" to cause people suffering.

When the disciples asked why the man was blind, Jesus said, "So that the works of God could be made manifest." The word *manifest* in the Greek carries the meaning that "it is not the cause."

What Jesus is saying here is "Guys, it doesn't matter who sinned. This isn't necessarily about the sin, it's about the glory of God. We are not really concerned about who broke it. Let's just get it fixed."

Jesus spat in the clay, made some mud, and anointed his eyes. *Anoint* means to rub in. He rubbed the wet clay into the eyes of the blind man, and He said, "Now I want you to go and wash in the pool called Siloam," which means "sent." The man obeyed, and verse 7 says he "came back seeing."

Now some people said, "Hey, we know that guy. Isn't he blind? Look at him, he looks like he sees." And another said, "No, that's not him. It just looks like him."

The man overheard and said, "It's me, it's really me."

They asked, "What happened?"

He replied, "A man named Jesus came by." He told them what had happened and said, "This is what I know. I once was blind, but now I see."

Then the church folks heard the man's story, and they said, "Wait a minute. This Jesus who healed you is a sinner, because He did it on the Sabbath." Why is that the religious folks want to take away all the good things that God wants to give you?

The others said, "How could this Jesus be a sinner when he does such wonderful things?" There is now some division among them. They decide to settle the issue.

The Jews said, "We don't believe the guy was ever blind in the first place. We want some proof for these miracles." They did a background check, and they found the man's parents.

I believe his parents knew that Jesus had healed him. Verses 19-21 say—

"… Is this your son, who you say was born blind? How then does he now see?"

His parents answered them and said, "We know that this is our son, and that he was born blind;

"but by what means he now sees we do not know, or who opened his eyes we do not know. He is of age; ask him. He will speak for himself."

The man was probably thinking, "Come on, Mom and Dad." But I want you to know why his parents did this. Look at verse 22. .

His parents said these things because they feared the Jews, for the Jews had agreed already that if anyone confessed that He was Christ, he would be put out of the synagogue.

What happened here? His parents were involved at the synagogue. Maybe they were greeters or something. For love of their tradition and for fear of being bumped out of their religious comfort zone, they weren't willing to be misunderstood. In a sense, they betrayed their son.

I believe they knew that Jesus had healed their son, but because of their fear, they were unwilling to be truthful witnesses that He was the Christ. See what fear did? Sometimes, because of fear, you won't stand up and say, "This is what I believe."

The religious leaders called the man in again and asked, "How did this happen?"

He said, "I already told you guys, a couple of times. You want so much information, do you want to become a disciple?" That's what he said, right there in verse 27.

They said, "No, you're His disciple. We're Moses' disciples." It went on until they threw the man out. Then Jesus came back and asked him, "Do you believe that I am the Christ?"

He said, "I believe." And he fell down and worshipped Jesus.

Now his parents missed out. Mom and Dad missed out because they feared, and because they feared they wouldn't say what they believed. I wonder what would have happened if they had said, "Yes, this is our son, and yes, he is blind from birth, and yes, Jesus the Christ healed him."

When the Jews said, "We're kicking you out of the synagogue," Mom and Dad would have said, "That's all right! We're going on our miracle parade."

Be fearless. Fear will paralyze you. Fear will even keep you from saying what you know to be true and what you believe. We find in Romans 8:15 that fear makes you a slave.
   "For you did not receive the spirit of bondage again to fear, but you received the Spirit of adoption by whom we cry out, 'Abba, Father.'"

Fear is bondage. Fear is very, very powerful. Fear wreaks havoc, especially in your mind. You probably know that to be true. Because it is so powerful, and it does such damage to lives, it requires a threefold remedy to repair and restore what it affects. The Word of God gives us the solution, which takes care of everything involved.

In Second Timothy 1:7 we read,
"For God has not given us a spirit of fear, but of power and of love and of a sound mind."

The first thing you need to do if you are experiencing fear is to recognize this is not from God. Then realize what God did give you.

In the Amplified Bible it reads—
For God did not give us a spirit of timidity (of cowardice, of craven and cringing and fawning fear), but [He has given us a spirit] of power and of love and of calm and well-balanced mind and discipline and self-control.

The spirit of fear, or spirit of bondage, is from the devil, and in response to that, God gives us the spirit of power, love, and a sound mind. If someone has a bad spirit, it creates a force around them. It can be an attitude, it can be an atmosphere—that is a spirit. God gives us a triple force that can overpower that spirit of fear. Understand this: the source of the force is the Holy Spirit.

When the spirit of fear comes, it devastates spirit, soul, and body. If you are living in fear, it plagues your mind. That's the first place it affects. It is kicking holes in the wall of your mind. It is pulling down things—beautiful things that were set up in your mind. Fear destroys them.

Then it works on your body. Your stomach begins to lock up. You breathe from only the top 10 percent of your lungs. Your blood pressure goes sky high. You become a grump. You get agitated. You get irritated. It will shut you down physically.

Spiritually, if you are operating in fear, you are going to have a hard time praying, and you are going to have a hard time believing. You are going to have a hard time worshiping. You are going to have a hard time getting into the Word. You are going to have a hard time even getting to church.

So what has to happen here? God comes in and says, "I did not give you the spirit of fear, but I have given you the spirit of power." What does the power do? The power is the result of His glory, of His presence. It will heal your body, it will change your situation. It will knock out that enemy. Glory!

Then God says, "And I have given you the spirit of love." First John 4:18 says, *"... Perfect love casts out fear."* It's going to take care of your mind, too, with calmness, discipline, and self-control.

So God gives a three-way remedy here. He says, I have given you power. I have given you love. I have given you a sound mind. Why? So you can be fearless!

In Mark 4:35-41, Jesus had just finished some more miracles and wonderful teaching. The disciples hopped into a boat, and Jesus said, "Let's go to the other side." He was tired after ministering, so He went below deck and lay down on a pillow. He went to sleep, and suddenly a storm arose.

The first thing the disciples were upset about wasn't the storm, but the audacity of Jesus to sleep. The wind and the waves were hitting them, and all they could think about was, "That Jesus is sleeping!" They paraded down into the lower part of the boat, and they said, "Jesus! Wake up! Don't you even care that we're about to perish?"

Jesus didn't say anything at that point, but He must have thought, "These guys just don't get it." He went up top. He still didn't say anything to them. Now notice this. He *rebuked* the wind, and then He *spoke* to the waves.

You may have circumstances just crashing in around you, and you are yelling at your waves. You're yelling at your kids, and your spouse, and your co-workers, and you're upset about all these other things that are rocking and splashing you, but that's not the source. You have to be source-minded.

Jesus stood up and rebuked the storm, and then He spoke to the waves, saying, "Peace, be still!" Men and women of God need to stand up and rebuke the storm and then declare, "Peace, be still!" to our waves.

Think about these disciples. They went and woke Him up and were a little agitated at Him, and now He stops the storm. It says they were fearful because He did that. Then He turned around, and they must have thought, "Oh God, He's coming for me."

But He said, *"Why are you so fearful? How is it that you have no faith?"* Another translation for the second question says, "What happened to your faith?"

Why are you so fearful? Here the word *fearful* in the Greek contains as its very definition "faithless." *When you are fearful, you are faithless.* In case you didn't get that: When you are fearful, you are faithless.

You cannot carry a problem and a promise at the same time. Some of you load up with your problems, and then get your little promise book. You are waiting for God to help you out. You can't carry them both. You have to decide, "Hey, get this trash off me." Take hold of the promises. You cannot be in fear and in faith at the same time.

Jesus asked, "Why are you so fearful? What happened to your faith?" The disciples had dismissed faith because they had were relying on the senses, looking and seeing what was happening. The circumstance was a very real circumstance, but they needed to operate in faith.

Why are we talking about being fearless? So that we can have *preservation and increase* in our lives.

Fear and faith are opposites, but they use the same principles. Think of a number line, a continuum. Right in the very center is zero. If you go to the right of that, it's positive. That's the direction of faith. If you go to the left, that's negative, and that's the direction of fear.

On that number line you use the same principles and the same laws, and you choose which direction you are going. Initially it requires the same effort to be in faith or to be in fear. They use the same principles, but faith and fear are opposites.

One of the principles is *confession*. Confession is saying what you believe. Confession for us is to say the same thing that God says. So in faith or fear, you use confession.

You listen to some people, and you can immediately identify where they are. You can locate if they're in fear or if they're in faith by what they say. They are saying what they believe. Fear is the perversion, the negative, of faith.

The spirit of faith is, "I believe and therefore I speak." (2 Cor. 4:13.) The reverse of the spirit of faith, the perversion of the spirit of faith, is the same thing: "I believe, therefore I speak." So whether you are in faith or in fear, you will confess it.

Some people don't want to get out of fear. Their explanation is, "I don't want to get over into that 'faith stuff,' if I've got to do confession."

You're doing it anyway, brother. The principles are the same. You've got to decide which way you want to go with them.

Someone asked me, "You're not one of these positive confession churches, are you?"

I said, "We sure are." But let me explain something. We also believe that there is a road and there are ditches. On one side is the Ditch of Excess and Abuse. On the other side is the Ditch of Avoidance.

People in the Ditch of Avoidance say, "It doesn't matter what you say. It doesn't matter what you say. I don't need to worry about what I say." But look at their lives.

Back in the first ditch, the hyperfaiths are chanting,"My nose is not running. My nose is not running. My nose is not running."

I want to say "Brother, your nose is running, and you need a Kleenex."

Now before you can have a Savior, you have to confess your need for a Savior. But when it comes to problems, you don't hold onto the confession of your problem, or to the denial of your problem. You hold onto the confession of your hope.

Up here on the Road of Truth, you say, "Lord, my nose is running, but I know that I am redeemed from this. Pass me a Kleenex, please. You are my Healer, and You Yourself carried away my sickness and disease. By Your stripes I am healed. The same Spirit that raised Jesus from the dead dwells in my body and quickens my mortal body. That Spirit makes me healthy, whole, and alive. And so I thank you for it, Lord.

"And here is a believer over here. Believer, will you lay hands on me? The Bible says that if you lay hands on the sick, they do recover. I believe that, and so I am going to recover."

Then you blow your nose, and you keep thanking God that you are healed.

"Well, how long do you keep thanking Him, saying you are healed?" Actually, forever. Before and after your healing, you thank Him for it. Quit quitting. Faith or fear, it involves confession.

The second principle of both faith and fear is *consistency.* You walk by faith, you live by faith. Or you can walk by fear and live by fear. This ties in with confession too.

A couple of years ago, I was at swimming lessons with my son. I was the only one in the bleachers named "Daddy." There should be more daddies at swimming lessons. I was sitting there watching my son, and there were some mothers there. I knew they were "church ladies," because they had been talking about vacation Bible school.

Then one began to talk about her little Suzie, out there swimming. She said, "Every year when swimming starts, little Suzie gets those ear infections. And it gets worse every year. All my kids have had it, and every year it gets worse. I just know today it will probably start."

Now did Mama want that for her? No. But she has learned to operate in a fear which involved her confession. Instead of overcoming it, she was allowing it to reign in their lives. It's up to you: faith or fear.

Another principle that faith and fear have in common is *meditation*. The Bible talks about meditation in Joshua 1, Psalm 1, and Psalm 119. Meditation means "to mutter to oneself." It literally comes from the idea of a cow chewing the cud. It means you are continually bringing what you have swallowed back up and chewing on it.

We are to meditate on the Word of God, day and night. You can also choose to meditate on the problem, day and night.

Faith and fear operate on the same principles. Faith and fear both come by hearing. Faith comes by hearing the word of God. Fear comes by hearing the problem.

These two kinds of believing have related, yet opposite results. In faith you overcome; in fear you are overcome. In faith you cast your cares; in fear you carry your cares. In faith you enter into rest; in fear there is no rest. In faith you enlarge your borders; in fear you shrink back. With faith, you please God; in fear you cannot please God.

Get ready for this. Faith calls those things that are not as though they are, Fear also calls those things that are not as though they are. Faith gives substance to the thing you hoped for. Fear gives substance to the thing you dread. Faith puts you in a posture and expectation to receive good from God. Fear puts you in a posture and expectation to receive bad from the devil.

Faith and fear are opposites, yet they work on the same principles. You have a choice about it all. Eventually fear will rot you. Fear will decay you from the inside out. It will take your heart right out of you. Job 3:25, 26 says—

For the thing I greatly feared has come upon me, And what I dreaded has happened to me.

I am not at ease, nor am I quiet. I have no rest, for trouble comes.

That doesn't sound like preservation and increase. Job 30:15 confirms it.

"Terrors are turned upon me; They pursue my honor as the wind, And my prosperity has passed like a cloud."

Job had fixed his thoughts on fear and dread, and that gave the opening to lose the blessing God had given. You have to get into faith—and that's not religion, either.

What is faith? Faith is that I am so convinced of God and so convinced of His Word, it becomes the highest truth in my life. I'll hear it, I'll speak it, I'll act on it, and it will be as God has said to me.

When Jesus came up on the deck during the storm, what was the advantage that He had? He knew the Father. That is the epitome of faith. He knew the character of the Father. He knew the power and the truth that was behind the Father, and so He rebuked the storm—fearlessly.

He rebuked the wind, and he hushed the waves. Then He asked, "What happened to your faith?" We have to get over into faith.

Quit dilly-dallying back and forth, and get on over into faith. Fear will rip you up. Fear wants to destroy you. You might say,"But what about this situation, and this situation?" That's going back to "Who sinned, his mom or his dad?"

"I don't even care, let's just fix it!"

"But something happened to me in third grade!" Well, I'm sorry that something happened to you, but do you really want to lose the rest of your life because of third grade? You have to get on over into faith.

I am so tired of hearing of "dysfunctional" and "co-dependent." Let's get *functional* and *dependent*. It can almost become a cop-out. "Well, something happened to me. I think when my mom was changing my diaper she poked me with a safety pin." God help us.

I'm not making light, if you had some rough things happen in your life. But don't get strapped in and locked in by little labels.

You need to get over in Christ, and you need to get over in faith. It's time to start saying, "Old things are passed away and, behold, all things become new. And I'm not dysfunctional; I'm functional.

And I'm not co-dependent on anything but God, and I'm totally dependent on Him." Get out of fear and get on over into faith.

"But, I have these fear thoughts." You need to have faith thoughts then, because faith overcomes. Quit speaking out all those fear words. Speak faith words! Let your actions not be fear actions, but faith actions. Faith overcomes.

Now I am going to give you six words, and if you don't learn anything else, these six words will float your boat.

Look at Isaiah 41:10-13.

Fear not, for I am with you; Be not dismayed, for I am your God. I will strengthen you, Yes, I will help you, I will uphold you with My righteous right hand.

Behold, all those who were incensed against you Shall be ashamed and disgraced; They shall be as nothing, And those who strive with you shall perish.

You shall seek them and not find them—Those who contended with you. Those who war against you Shall be as nothing, As a nonexistent thing.

For I, the Lord your God, will hold your right hand, Saying to you,...

Here are the six words: *"'Fear not, I will help you.'"*

That's all that you need to know. "I have a job interview." *Fear not, I will help you.* "I've got a doctor's appointment." *Fear not, I will help you.* "I've got some bills here." *Fear not, I will help you.* I don't care what it is. He said, "Fear not, I will help you."

That's all you need to know. Since when did you think that you could do it single-handed, anyway? You need help. I need help.

Fear not, I will help you. So get out of fear. Break those things off of your life. You almost have to get mad with it. Step on over into faith, and stay in faith, and let it take you on over into victory, preservation, and increase!

12

He Preserves the Faithful

Key No. 10 is *faithfulness.*

Psalm 31:23 reads, ***"Oh, love the Lord, all you His saints! For the Lord preserves the faithful."*** The Lord preserves the faithful. *Preserve* there means "guard, protect, and maintain." The Lord preserves the faithful. So another key to preservation and increase, another key to playing for keeps, another key to restoration, is *faithfulness.*

If you will be faithful, God will preserve you, He will guard you, He will protect you, and He will maintain you.

First Corinthians 4:2 in the Amplified Bible declares,
> ***"Moreover, it is [essentially] required of stewards that a man should be found faithful [proving himself worthy of trust]."***

Did you know that you are a steward? Now, it is required of you that you be found faithful.

Let's say you want to be a doctor, and you decide that you don't want to take anatomy. No, I'm sorry; that's a required subject. If a teacher gives you required reading and suggested reading, guess what list you should start on first? Required reading. Do you know what that means? You are not going to get through this without it.

So it is required of a steward that he be found faithful, that he is proven to be worthy of trust. Proverbs 25:19 reads,

"Confidence in an unfaithful man in time of trouble is like a bad tooth."

No one enjoys a bad tooth. In case you've forgotten what it's like, wad up a little piece of tin foil and just chew on it for a minute. That will remind you.

It's even worse than that. *"Confidence in an unfaithful man in time of trouble is like a bad tooth and a foot out of joint."* A while back my wife, Alicia, and our son, Lee, had gone somewhere, and I was home. I was in charge of Joshua, who was two at the time, and our little girl Alyce, who was four. I had to change Joshua's diaper, and I think that all daddies should change diapers. If you didn't do it as a daddy, do it when you're a grandpa. It's good for you.

My wife and I have a rule, anyway. The rule is "finders keepers." We have a very honest relationship, so I can't say, "Um, (sniff) honey, do you want to hold the baby?" She will hand him right back.

This day, I needed to change Joshua, and so I went in his room and grabbed a diaper and one of the little wipes. When I came out, Joshua was by the fireplace. I pulled his little diaper off, and, well, his little system was out of balance. So I thought, "Oh, I have a mess." I was holding up his little legs and trying to use that one wipe. I've just got a major mess, and he's twisting around. So I hollered out to my little girl, "Alyce, Alyce!"

She said, "Yes, Daddy."

"I need you to come help me."

"OK, Daddy."

Joshua is squirming, and we have a mess here. It's about to get on the carpet and everything else. "Alyce, Daddy needs you."

"OK, Daddy."

"Right now. I need you right now! Come here right now."

So finally she came out. "Yes, Daddy?"

"I need some baby wipes. We have a problem here, and I need you to go and get the whole thing of baby wipes."

"OK, Daddy." She walked on, and she turned the wrong way and went back to her room to play.

"Confidence in an unfaithful man in time of trouble is like a bad tooth and a foot out of joint."

Notice, it said in time of trouble. Nobody takes joy in an unfaithful helper. Faithfulness is the cornerstone of character. That means your character is built upon the fact that you are faithful. If you are not faithful, you don't have much character.

A man's name is only as good as his word. Read that again. A man's name is only as good as his word. Some people by their word prove their character, either way.

That is why we can trust Father God, because He has proven His character. What is His character? He's faithful. This has been such a rich revelation in my life. Yes, He's my Healer, He's my Savior, He's my Provider, He's my Comforter, He's my Counselor, He's my Helper, He's my Protector, but more than that, He's faithful. If He weren't faithful, I couldn't count on His being any of the rest of those things. So faithfulness is the cornerstone of character.

Now this will free you today, too. God is more interested in your character than in your conduct. Have you ever gone a whole week and not made a mistake? How many times have you blown it, but your heart was right, and you had the best intentions? God looks on your performance, but, more closely, God looks on your heart.

I'm not a perfect pastor, but I have a heart after God, and God knows my heart. I might come short in a lot of different areas, but God knows my heart. God is more interested in your character than in your conduct. That should free you up.

God won't trust you with what you want, if He can't trust you with what you have. Some people say, "I want a car. God, bless me with a car. Please bless me with a car."

"Well, don't you have a car?"

"Yeah, that old rattletrap."

"Why don't you wash it? I haven't seen McDonald's bags like those on your floorboard for years. They're a collector's item. Why don't you put a little oil in it? Why don't you be faithful with what you have?"

The scripture says in Luke 16 that if you are faithful in little, then God can trust you with more. If you are faithful with another man's possessions, then He can trust you with your own. God won't trust you with what you want, if He can't trust you with what you have.

Remember, we are talking about *faithfulness* as a key to preservation and increase. First Timothy 1:12 reads,

"And I thank Christ Jesus our Lord who has enabled me, because He counted me faithful, putting me into the ministry."

The Amplified Bible says,

"... granted me the needed strength and made me able for this."

It's because He counts you faithful that He will enable you, and then ministry will follow. There are people who seek ministry and seek ability, but won't be faithful. But, you have got to be faithful, and when God counts you faithful, He will put you in a place of ministry.

In Second Timothy 2:2 we read,

"And the things that you have heard from me among many witnesses, commit these to faithful men who will be able to teach others also."

Look at this. What does the world do? The world commits to "able" men and doesn't care if they're faithful. They'll commit a multimillion-dollar contract to a ballplayer who has ability. He can jump high, or run fast, or throw a ball, or hit long or whatever. But he doesn't have faithfulness, and he hasn't developed character yet.

With all that money, because he doesn't have character, it consumes and destroys him. Our society is kind of backwards.

I enjoy watching a ballgame, but, as wonderful as the players are in their sport, somehow I think the world would be a lot better—just in terms of having values in the right place—if that were their part-time job. Wealth is so unevenly distributed. What about teachers, and what about nurses, police, and firemen? What about people who do things that are helping folks? Faithfulness—we must commit to faithfulness. Then they will be able to carry out God's purpose.

I recently read the testimony of a man named Norm. Norm had a wife and three girls, and he had an upper-level management position in a large corporation. One day his supervisor told him that because of a financial situation, he had to be let go. After 20 years with this company—a good income and good benefits, so that he was sole provider for his family—suddenly everything was gone.

Norm not only applied spiritual principles but natural common-sense principles as well. He had heard his pastor say that you should spend as much time looking for a job as you would spend working. He said, "I knew that the Lord had a job out there for me. I just had to keep believing and looking."

The family thought the unemployment would last about 30 days, and surely he would be able to find a job. It ended up being nine agonizing, long months.

Then one day Norm saw a help-wanted sign in the window of a Subway Sandwich Shop. It was a part-time job that paid $4.25 per hour. When he walked in to apply, little did he realize that this was

God's answer to his prayer. Norm started out as a crew person making sandwiches. Remember, this is a former executive. His shift manager was a 15-year-old high school girl.

Within two months, he was promoted to a management position, which doubled his pay. Later, he was moved up to a supervisory position. Finally, after a little over a year, he was made operations manager over six stores.

Looking back, Norm and his family realized that God had answered their prayers. They hadn't expected that the $4.25-an-hour job would eventually become God's provision for them. In fact, they are now better off financially than when he lost his first job. Confident in God, Norm said, "I no longer believe God's word works, now I *know* it works."

What is the key that he applied? *Faithfulness.* It didn't take any time at all for God to reward Norm's faithfulness and bring that about in his life.

Jesus gave an example in Matthew 25:14-30. It begins—
> ***For the kingdom of heaven is like a man traveling to a far country, who called his own servants and delivered his goods to them.***
> ***And to one he gave five talents, to another two, and to another one, to each according to his own ability; and immediately he went on a journey....***

When he came back, he said to the one with five talents, "Show me what you have done with it."

He said, "I invested it, and I put the money to work, and now it's ten talents."

The lord and master said, "Well done, good and faithful servant. Enter into the joy."

Then he went to the one he had given two talents and he said, "Show me what you did."

He said, "I did this with it, and I did this with it, and I doubled it."

And he said, "Well done, good and faithful servant. Enter into the joy." Faithfulness brings you to the point of joy.

Then he asked the one who had received one talent.

This man took two whole verses to explain why he had done nothing. He said, "Here it is." Notice something here that is true in life. Usually those who do the least talk the most.

The lord said, ***"You wicked, lazy servant,"*** and scolded him severely. He went on to say, ***"For to everyone who has, more will be given, and he will have abundance; but from him who does not have, even what he has will be taken away."***

Everyone who has or does not have what? Faithfulness. Faithfulness results in abundance. Faithfulness results in preservation and increase. Unfaithfulness results in loss. Unfaithfulness results in losing what you do have. So the spiritual truth to be learned here is faithfulness.

In Malachi 3:11, God says, ***"And I will rebuke the devourer for your sakes."*** For whose sake? For you, if you are faithful.

Be faithful.

13

You Can Have What You Say

The eleventh key is *confession*. You need to get these keys, so to speak, on your spiritual key ring. These are the keys to preservation and increase. I don't know anybody who wouldn't want preservation and increase, if he really knew it could be his.

Hebrews 11:3 reads,

"By faith we understand that the worlds were framed by the word of God, so that the things which are seen were not made of things which are visible."

That holds a lot of hope right there. Maybe you have a situation where you don't see any way out. What does God do? He makes things that are seen out of things that are not seen. So even though you can't see the solution, you should rejoice in this: God does see the solution. He sees what it's going to take to bring it together.

By faith, we understand that the worlds were framed by the Word of God. The literal translation is "the whole scheme of time and space"—everything—was framed by the Word of God. *Framed* here translates this way: "fitted, formed, and prepared."

Whether you understand it or not, whether you believe it or not, God spoke things into existence. He said, "Light, be," and light was. He said, "Water, be," and water was. God spoke, and it was created. How did He do that? By His Word.

Men waste a lot of time trying to figure how some planets exploded, and then some gaseous vapors all got together and made a pond. Then the pond developed some scum, and from that scum, we have us. I am insulted. We were made in the likeness and image of God, on purpose. God made you and me on purpose. God created. He spoke it, and it was.

The Bible says that He spoke it, and it stood fast. It was framed by the Word of God. One translation says, "… created, beautifully coordinated, and now exists at God's command." Another says, "The world came into being by the command of God's Word."

God spoke, and there it was. Hebrews 1:3 says,

> *"Who being the brightness of His glory and the express image of His person, and upholding all things by the word of His power."*

God created everything, framed everything, fitted, prepared, and formed everything by His spoken Word. Now we find in Hebrews 1:3 that He *upholds* the things that He created.

Remember we are talking about playing for keeps, and about preservation and increase. The good things that you have in your life came from God. They came into your life, and now, by the Word of God, you are also able to uphold those things.

It says here again, *"… upholding all things by the word of His power."* The Amplified Bible says,

> *"… upholding and maintaining and guiding and propelling the universe, by His mighty word of power."*

"Word," in both of these verses in Hebrews—the Word that framed the worlds, and the Word that upholds the universe—is the translation of *rhema* in the Greek. *Rhema* is the spoken, living, active Word of God. God spoke, and things happened.

Understand this. God's Word contains God's power. I want you to read that again. *God's Word contains God's power.* That power is released when the Word of God is spoken. I pray you will get this today.

God's Word contains God's power, and that power is activated when it is spoken in faith. If it were released when it is only written, then all we would have to do is cover the earth with tracts. We could fly over heathen tribes and just litter them with leaflets. That would take care of them.

But the Word is released when it is spoken. You weren't born again until you came in line with the Word of God. Actually, you weren't born again until you *said* you were. It happened when you believed in your heart that Jesus died for you and God raised Him from the dead, and then you spoke with your mouth and said, "Jesus is Lord." That's the highest truth. Jesus is Lord.

When you did that, a miracle took place, and power was turned loose to cause your spirit to be reborn. That happened only because you opened your mouth and said that Jesus is Lord.

Do you see why the devil likes to have religion keep you quiet? "Pray to yourself, silently." No! God's Word contains God's power, and the power is released when it is spoken.

In John 6:63, did Jesus say, "... The words that I *think* to you"? No, He said, ***"The words that I speak to you are spirit, and they are life."*** So when I take the words that Jesus spoke to me, they

147

release to me spirit, which is power, and they release to me life, which is the very life of God.

Here's some good news and some bad news, from Proverbs 18:20 in the Amplified Bible.

"A man's [moral] self shall be filled with the fruit of his mouth; and with the consequences of his words he must be satisfied, [whether good or evil].

Death and life are in the power of the tongue, and they who indulge in it shall eat the fruit of it [for death or life]"

Notice something here. It says that you shall be filled with the fruit of *your* mouth. Not the fruit of another's mouth. I don't care what people speak over me, because my life is not filled with the fruit of their mouths. It is filled with the fruit of mine. You say, "But I see people whose lives were affected by other people's words." That's because they took them as their own.

Your life will be filled with the outgrowth of things you have said. You need to be careful about the words that you align yourself with. Look at it again:

"...and with the consequences of his words he must be satisfied [whether good or evil]."

Now here is the bad news. Life is composed of choices and constructed by words, and your life right now is the product of your choices and your words.

"Oh, no, no. Somebody else messed this up for me."

Oh, no, no. Your life is composed of choices and constructed by words. The Bible says,

> ***"Death and life are in the power of the tongue, and they who indulge in it shall eat the fruit of it [for death or life]."***

You see, religion always likes to give us an excuse to explain away our failure. "Oh, God must have changed His mind." Or, "God's on a lottery system." They want to rationalize why things aren't happening quite right in our lives, but, honestly, life is composed of our choices. Eternity is decided by your choice. Your life is constructed by your words. Choices and words. Proverbs 6:2 says that you are snared by the words of your mouth. Choices and words.

You choose your words, too. Has anybody ever made you say something? I can only think of one time, and that was because my big brother was holding me down. You decide what you are going to say. The Bible says that in the abundance of words there wanteth not for sin. (Prov. 10:19.) If you just feel like you need to talk, I guarantee you that you are probably going to sin. Sometimes, one of the strongest things that you can do is to be silent.

Now those choices and those words are going to uphold, or they are going to undermine. *Undermine* actually means "to dig out underneath." Do you know what will happen? Whatever is supporting you will collapse, and you will be swallowed.

Proverbs 14:1 says,

> ***"The wise woman builds her house, But the foolish one pulls it down with her hands."***

In every situation, you can build up and uphold—or you can tear down and undermine. Either you can cause death, or you can cause life.

149

Faith-filled words will put you over. Fear-filled words will defeat you. *Words are the most powerful thing in the universe.*

In our legal system, all court cases are based on words. Stenographers are there transcribing every word. I never have figured out those little machines. They only have about eight buttons, and yet they can write down everything you say. Do you think they're faking?

For any kind of purchase, you have to have contracts or deeds . What is that? Words. You capture spoken words on paper, so that they can be recalled again in a spoken form.

Words are the most powerful thing in the universe. We must get hold of this, that our words contain the power of death and life.

If we want preservation and increase, we have to learn to speak God's words and release God's power into our situations. Instead of undermining, we can uphold by our choices and by our words.

In Hebrews 10:23 we read,
"Let us hold fast the confession of our hope without wavering, for He who promised is faithful."

"Hold fast" there reminds me of that bulldog. We must not let go. Some translations render that a confession of "hope," some render it "faith." In this verse the substance is the same. We keep on declaring our belief in the thing that we desire, because God will do what He said.

Faith gives substance to that thing that you hope for. (Heb. 11:1.) However, some people would rather hold fast to the confession of their dread. They will speak harm and death over

150

their finances, their business, or their health. "Our business is just going to go completely down the drain." ... "I always get sick in January." Others take everybody else's report and make it their own. They will defend it, even if you try to point out that they are undermining what they have set their hand to do.

"How?"

"By your words."

No wonder some people work themselves into the grave. They apply all their own energy and strength, but then they speak powerful words of death to tear down what they are working on. It's a horrible, horrible cycle.

But we're to hold fast to the confession, not of our dread but of our hope and our faith. Don't let go of that. That word *confession* there is actually from two Greek words, which mean "the same words." It's "to say the same thing."

Our confession of hope, or our confession of faith, comes from the Word of God. We say the same thing as God says regarding our situation.

Some may say, "You can't say God's words. You're acting like God." I'd rather say God's words and be an imitator of God than say the devil's words and act like the devil. Do you want words of life or do you want words of death? It's up to you.

Remember, God's power is released when we speak God's Word.

Mark 11:23 reads,

"For assuredly, I say to you, that whoever says to this mountain, 'Be removed and be cast into the sea,' and does not doubt in his heart, but believes that those things he says will be done, he will have whatever he says."

Now, you need to be careful with your words.

"Oh, no. Last night I watched something on TV and I said, 'I think I'm going to laugh my head off.'" I don't really think your head is going to come off, but why would you say that?

What do you believe? You must believe that the things you say are going to come to pass. Can you do that? Absolutely.

Jesus taught His disciples, "You will have what you say." Some people fight this, but Jesus said it. Whether you can figure it out or not, it is truth. And whether you like it or not, it will work.

Say, "I can have what I say." Your life will be filled with the fruit of your words and with the consequences of your mouth. Death and life are in the power of the tongue. It is going to be in your future.

Let me mention something here. Any point is a turning point. You can be heading on toward the great things of God, just full of peace and joy and victory, every need met. But you must be careful, and take heed, lest when you think you stand, you fall. (1 Cor. 10:12.) Any point is a turning point.

It works the other way, too. You can be going down the drain, everything apparently falling apart, things looking worse and worse. Any point is a turning point. Speak life into your situation.

Jesus said if you will believe that those things you say will come to pass, you can have what you say. And that works positively or negatively. Let me give you a couple of examples.

In the church that I pastor, we continually declare that God is taking us from glory to glory. We know that what we say will come to pass. As long as our church has been around, every newsletter ever published and every tape ever recorded has me saying, "Glory to glory."

And truly, God has already taken us from glory to glory. He continues taking us from glory to glory. Do you know the wonderful thing about that? Each succeeding glory is so great that it swallows up the previous glory. Isn't that incredible?

I believe that with all my heart. So do I just think about it? No, I speak it. We as a church speak it. And we're not going from "gory to gory," either. We're going from glory to glory.

I speak "summer bump" and not "summer slump." A church that has me on their mailing list sent me a letter last June, saying, "As you know, it's time for 'summer slump.'" They enclosed a stack of offering envelopes. Do you know what motivated that? Fear.

You can go back and check, and every summer, since the beginning of our church, I have said, "summer bump." Every year, we have had summer bump. I think I might upgrade it this year to "summer jump."

Does something go wrong in the Kingdom of God in the summer? Are some promises "closed for summer" or "gone fishing"? Do the angels go on vacation? What is the deal? No, it is still all ours.

Some church leaders decide, "It's all going to fall apart for the summer, anyway. Might as well shut it down." At the church where I grew up, they cut back in summer to nothing except the Sunday morning service. Then one week they would have an arts and crafts festival. Do you know what I made at church in the arts and crafts festival as a child? A thing like an ashtray, with a fern in it.

You can say, "I'm blessed." Or you can say, "I'm broke." You can say, "This is going to be the best Sunday we ever had." Or you can say, "Let's just wait and see what happens." You can say, "My children will serve God." Or you can say, "Well, you know, they all rebel."

Why does your life have to be filled with the fruit of other people's words? God's Word contains God's power, and that power is released when we speak His Word.

Let's look at the spirit of faith. Second Corinthians 4:13 says, *"And since we have the same spirit of faith, according to what is written, 'I believed and therefore I spoke,' we also believe and therefore speak."*

What is the spirit of faith? You speak what you believe.

Some people just speak what they think. You'd better be careful of that. Jesus said that out of the abundance of the heart the mouth speaks. (Luke 6:45.) Some people give themselves away because they say, "I'm just this type of person. I've got to speak what's on my mind." They are revealing what is the treasure of their heart.

That's why Proverbs 17:28 says that sometimes it's best just to stay quiet. Even a fool is perceived to be wise, as long as he keeps his mouth shut. What do we do? We open our mouths and remove all doubt. You speak what you believe. What you believe had better be founded on the Word of God, or you don't have a leg to stand on.

What is it about God's Word? God's Word contains God's power. When I speak or confess what I believe, based on the Word, it brings results.

Say this out loud: "I believe in my heart, and I speak what I believe. I believe that those things I speak will come to pass, and I have what I say."

So a very important key to preservation and increase is your words. They are death, or they are life. They are upholding, or they are undermining. Your life will be filled with the fruit of your mouth and with the consequences of your words, whether good or evil.

You have the choice. Your life is composed of the choices to speak God's Word containing God's power, and that power is released when you speak it. So speak the Word of God. Believe it and speak it—over your family, over your health, over your finances.

You may say, "But there is nothing to speak over." Well, God can make things out of what is not seen. It's easy to agree with what you see. "Yup, that's a big hole in the road." That's easy, but we don't walk by sight, we walk by faith. And there is no such thing as quiet faith. Faith always speaks.

Jesus said if you have faith as a mustard seed, you will *say.* (Matt. 17:20.) Faith people speak what they believe. They believe that what they speak will come to pass. And because of that, they have what they say.

14
The Blood of The Lamb

Key No. 12 is *apply the Blood.* I get excited every time I think about, hear about, sing about, or read about the Blood. There are religious movements that are removing the Blood. They're taking it out of their hymn books and their sermon books. They say that it's offensive, and it's not politically correct and not socially correct. But I want to tell you, it's spiritually correct.

Without the Blood, you might as well give it up. If we don't have the Blood, we are not born again. If we don't have the Blood, our hope of heaven and the Word is no good. Without the Blood, we are in big, big trouble.

Look at Revelation 12:11.

"And they overcame him by the blood of the Lamb and by the word of their testimony, and they did not love their lives to the death."

The faithful brothers in Christ had the victory over the devil. Jesus bought it with His blood. Notice how they kept it: with their confession and their commitment.

If you have been in Pentecostal or Full Gospel circles for years, you've always heard the phrase, "plead the Blood." But you must know what is behind that.

It's not the *truth* that sets you free. It's the truth that you *know* that sets you free. (John 8:32.) If you don't understand something, it's easy for it to be taken from you.

So we must grasp what applying the Blood or pleading the Blood really means. In John 10:10, "the thief" refers to the devil and also to false teachers. We're going to use it here to implicate the devil.

"The thief does not come except to steal, and to kill, and to destroy."

A thief takes what belongs to you. What is he always taking? Does the devil come in and take away your headache? Does the devil come in and take away the chaos? No, he only takes what God has given you, because they're the only things of worth.

He steals your peace. He steals your joy. He steals your health. He steals your finances. He tries to steal unity. He is always trying to take what belongs to you. If we are dealing in preservation and increase, we have to stop the devil from taking what belongs to us.

It is so important that you have a revelation of righteousness. It's not based on what you have done, but on Jesus. Your faith and your acceptance of what He did put you in right standing with God. You know you messed up. But because of what Jesus did, you have access to the Father, as if you never messed up.

"I can't understand that." You don't have to. Just accept it by faith.

Sin gives the devil leverage. Have you sinned this week? If you didn't sin, it was because you were sleeping all week, and if you slept all week, that's sin. But sin gives him leverage. It doesn't take away your righteousness, or your right standing. Instead, it takes away your *sense* of righteousness, because you have a conscience, and because Satan is the accuser of the brethren. So you are very aware of what you did wrong.

In most cases, when you sin, you meant to. It's rare that we sin and say, "Oops, I sinned." ... "Oops, I robbed that bank." ... "Oops, I punched that guy right in the nose." We hardly ever just happen to sin. Usually we know full well that we're doing it.

The point is that while we are here, we still have a great susceptibility to sin. However, that doesn't give us a license to sin.

Sin shall no longer have dominion over you. (Rom. 6:14.) You don't let it rule you. But when you do sin, it gives the devil an advantage. He comes in and toys with your emotions. If you lack knowledge of the Word of God, he'll set up a whole carnival right there on your dinner table.

What he does is to make you feel you can't confess that sin to God and receive forgiveness. Why? Because you have been there a thousand times before. So his first move is to keep you away from that place of restoration. You are still righteous, but you have to regain that sense of righteousness.

If he holds you back, you begin to pile up sin. Then he comes along with his little calculator and refigures your sin total. He says, "See? You're a slave to sin and bondage again under me." Some people fall back then under the lordship of the devil, when actually the Blood has delivered them out of the kingdom of darkness. They forget they've been translated into the kingdom of God's Son, who paid the price for the forgiveness of their sins. (Colossians 1:13, 14.)

You are no longer under Satan's control, but he keeps trying to talk you back into it. "You're a sinner. People of God don't do that, so you're not a child of God. I'm your lord again." See why you have to be "in the know"? You have to be in the know!

What can we do? First John 1:7-2:2 reads—

But if we walk in the light as He is in the light, we have fellowship with one another, and the blood of Jesus Christ His Son cleanses us from all sin.

If we say that we have no sin, we deceive ourselves, and the truth is not in us.

If we confess our sins, He is faithful and just to forgive us our sins and to cleanse us from all unrighteousness.

If we say that we have not sinned, we make Him a liar, and His word is not in us.

My little children, these things I write to you, so that you may not sin. And if anyone sins, we have an Advocate with the Father, Jesus Christ the righteous.

And He Himself is the propitiation for our sins, and not for ours only but also for the whole world.

Those sins have already been paid for. The Blood has already been shed, but I have to come back and confess. Remember, *confess* means to say the same thing. I have to admit to God that this was sin. "Lord, I fell short of Your glory, right here." By coming back into agreement with God and confessing that, I release again His power, and the power of His Word, and the power of the Blood to make me clean and to make me certain that the sin is washed away.

If we only knew. If we could only get a glimpse of the power of the blood of Jesus. In this lifetime, we will never have full understanding of it. But if we could just accept this as fact, that the blood of Jesus is enough to cleanse you of all sin.

Revelation 12:10 talks about the accuser of the brethren. He's the one coming around reminding you with his little calculator of your sin total. But the Blood silences the accuser.

In John 14:30, Jesus referred to the devil.
"... The ruler of this world is coming, and he has nothing in Me."

He had nothing in Jesus. No rights, no holds, no claims, no powers. The Amplified Bible says,
"... The prince (evil genius, ruler) of the world is coming. And he has no claim on me, he has nothing in common with Me, there is nothing in Me that belongs to him and he has no power over me."

The Blood has delivered me out of Satan's control. Because I've been set free and forgiven of my sins, then I can declare boldly to his face, "You have nothing *in* me, you have nothing *on* me, no claim on me, nothing in common with me. You have no rights to anything that I have and no power over me, because of the Blood. Not because of what I've done but because of the blood of Jesus!"

Hebrews 9:11-15 says—
But Christ came as High Priest of the good things to come, with the greater and more perfect tabernacle not made with hands, that is, not of this creation.

Not with the blood of goats and calves, but with His own blood, He entered the Most Holy Place once for all, having obtained eternal redemption.

For if the blood of bulls and goats and the ashes of a heifer, sprinkling the unclean, sanctifies for the purifying of the flesh,

how much more shall the blood of Christ, who through the eternal Spirit offered Himself without spot to God, cleanse your conscience from dead works to serve the living God?

And for this reason He is the Mediator of the new covenant.

Jesus, as our go-between, brought a sacrifice to God that was far more powerful than the animal sacrifices of the Old Testament. He was the priest, and He was the flawless offering. His blood was good enough to pay for the world's sins through ages to come.

One chapter back, in Hebrews 8:6, we see that by His blood He brought about something beyond what Moses had, or Abraham before him.

"But now He has obtained a more excellent ministry, inasmuch as He is also Mediator of a better covenant, which was established on better promises."

Did you know that Abraham had it made? He had it made. Guess what? We have a better covenant established on better promises. How? By the Blood.

Look in Hebrews 7:22.

"By so much more, Jesus has become a surety of a better covenant."

Jesus has become not only the mediator, but also the guarantee of the new covenant. Your redemption is secure. It is assured. That means He paid the price for your freedom, and nothing can take it away. Nobody can take it, if you understand who you are, where you are, and what belongs to you.

As you do that and take hold of your redemption, your new covenant rights are sealed by the blood of Jesus Himself. The surety or the guarantee of the new covenant is the Blood, and the essence of the new covenant is salvation.

Although we have made salvation very religious, it's a wonderful, wonderful, thing. Salvation is not *just* the forgiveness of sins. I am thankful for the forgiveness of sins. Unless you are born again and unless you are saved, you are in big trouble. You need to get that settled today. God loves you, and He made the way for the forgiveness of sins.

But I am so grateful that it is much more than the forgiveness of sins. What Jesus did gives us total salvation. The Greek word for *salvation* implies this as well. It is "deliverance"—that means rescue. Do you ever need rescue? It also means "safety, preservation, healing, soundness, and total redemption." Total redemption!

The guarantee of the new covenant is the Blood. And the essence of the new covenant is total redemption. Your total redemption is guaranteed by the Blood. Centuries before, as Exodus 12:21 says,

> **"Then Moses called for all the elders of Israel and said to them, 'Pick out and take lambs for yourselves according to your families, and kill the Passover lamb.'"**

First Corinthians 5:7 points out that Christ was our Passover, sacrificed for us. What happened in Egypt is the Old Testament type and shadow. Jesus has become the reality of that for us. Jesus is our Passover lamb. Remember, John the Baptist looked up and said,

> *"Behold! The Lamb of God who takes away the sin of the world!"* (John 1:29.)

Exodus 12:22, 23 continues God's instructions for Passover.

> *And you shall take a bunch of hyssop, dip it in the Blood that is in the basin, and strike the lintel and the two doorposts with the Blood that is in the basin. And none of you shall go out of the door of his house until morning.*
>
> *For the Lord will pass through to strike the Egyptians; and when He sees the Blood on the lintel and on the two doorposts, the Lord will pass over the door and not allow the destroyer to come into your houses to strike you.*

What kept him out? The Blood! By virtue of the Blood of the Passover lamb, the destroyer is not allowed to come into your house to strike you. This was a principle God wanted Israel to remember always.

> *"And you shall observe this thing as an ordinance for you and your sons forever."*

Christ is our Passover lamb, sacrificed for us. Ephesians 1:7 and Colossians 1:14 declare that we have redemption through His blood. We have total redemption, we have a new and better covenant, based upon better promises, and guaranteed by the Blood.

Let's look at exactly how to plead the Blood. In Exodus 12:22, you were to apply the lamb's blood to the lintel, which is the top piece of your door frame, and to the doorpost, the sides coming down. You were to daub the blood there with the cluster of hyssop.

This is the entrance to your house, which represents your covering. Underneath your covering are your home, your spouse, your children, your health, your finances, your business, your relationships, your future, your peace of mind. You name it.

When you apply the Blood, when you plead the Blood out loud, you proclaim what you have because of the Blood. You declare your redemptive rights, and you'd better know what they are. Over your family, over your relationships, over your health, over your home, over your safety, over your possessions, over your finances, over your business, over your church, over your ministry—you declare what the Word of God says that the Blood has purchased for you as a result of new covenant.

You may say, "How does this really work?" The Blood defeated the devil, and when you are in the know about that, basically what you're doing is drawing the Blood line. You can't go to the bookstore and buy blood. It is the spiritual application—by knowing that this belongs to you, that you are a child of God, bought by the Blood that sealed and guaranteed the covenant that keeps you.

"How often do you do this?"

You post it. It's like posting a sign that says, "No Trespassing." If you feel your sign is fading, repaint it. If you feel as if the outsider is not observing the fact that there is no trespassing, then you march up and down your border declaring what is rightfully yours.

Now, I want to go back to a strong principle. Remember, the devil cannot legally lay on you what God has already laid on His Son. The price has been paid. This is the end of the rip-off.

I hope you are getting this. It will make such a difference in your life. The result is that He will not allow the destroyer to come into your house to strike you.

Maybe you say, "I can see where it's been happening. I've been struck. The destroyer has been coming into my home." Then begin to plead the Blood. You begin to stand up again and to declare what is yours by virtue of the Blood covenant.

Will it work? Absolutely. What belongs to you? Everything in the new covenant. If you think Abraham was blessed in protection and provision and health, you have a better covenant, established on better promises. Guaranteed by the Blood. You don't have to go back every year and make another payment on it. It is paid for. It is done. It is settled.

And I want you to know this. The devil recognizes that fact. You have to recognize it, so you can enforce it. That's because he is a thief, and the way he steals from you is by talking you out of things. But if you know it, then declare it, mark it, post it "No Trespassing," plead the blood of Jesus, and walk in preservation and increase.

15
2-Way Communication

We are looking at keys to *preservation and increase.* The things of God do not come into our lives to break, wear out, or expire. God's benefits are to be preserved, maintained, and increased. They really aren't just for us. They are in our lives to be a blessing to somebody else. By these same keys, God will also work *restoration* in your life.

Psalm 34:8 says,
> *"Oh, taste and see that the Lord is good."*

If you get a good taste of the Lord, nothing else will satisfy. Nothing else will satisfy, anyway.

You need to know *who you are* in Jesus, *what you have* in Jesus, and *what you can do* in Jesus. You need to know what the Word says about you.

The next key is *Word and prayer levels.*

On the dashboard of your car, you have meters and instruments to monitor different things. If your car is overheating, or if you are running out of fuel, for example, they let you know about it.

Somebody gave a pastor friend of mine a car, a Chrysler 5th Avenue. It was one that talked. If you didn't get your door closed right, it would say, "A door is ajar." It said several things. We really got a kick out of that, because at the time neither one of us had a dollar to his name, but he had a car that talked.

We had started a church, and we were believing God and working hard. His wife was working in a bank, and my wife was working for the school board. We were doing everything that we could do to get that church up and running.

One day we were driving around doing visitation, and he said, "Hey, let's eat some lunch. Do you want to go by your house?"

I said, "There's not anything at my house."

So we went through the ashtray and under the seats, and finally we got enough money. We went to a Kentucky Fried Chicken. They had these little sandwiches called "Chicken Littles." So we bought a big Coke and two Chicken Littles. We had lunch and change left over. Praise God!

We had just bought that lunch, and the car started talking to us again. It said, "Fuel level low." Then we continue to drive, and it started talking a lot. "Fuel level low."

There are some indicators that you don't ignore. The van that we now drive has lights and indicators on the dash that show you what's happening. It calls all the doors "hatches" or "gates," and it will indicate, "Gate Open." Since we now have three children, if the indicator says "Gate Open," we stop and check it out. Or if it shows, "Fuel Level Low."

Ours doesn't talk. I don't want a car that talks. I've had a bad experience. But if it indicates, "Fuel Level Low," we start immediately considering what we need to do to get some fuel.

It has another indicator that says, "Washer Fluid Low." You know, I could drive to Canada and back, and I really don't care about that.

On our spiritual dashboard, some lights will come on to warn us about things that matter a lot. Our Word level and our prayer level are vital. It is almost like "Fuel Level Low."

We must be careful not to ignore the fact that our Word level or our prayer level might be low. If you want to play for keeps, you have to keep those levels up.

You may say, "Well, I don't necessarily feel like it."

That is not even an option. In your car, if the fuel gauge arrow is down on "E," that "E" stands for "Empty." If you continue on long enough, that "E" becomes a "W," for "Walk." Even if you don't feel like going to get fuel, you'd better.

When your Word level is low, and you ignore it, you're going to find yourself stranded somewhere. And if your prayer level is low, you might think that it's just depression or hunger. You cannot confuse these indicators that are in your spirit man, letting you know that your Word level and your prayer level are low.

If you are going to hold on to anything that God has brought into your life, you'd better have some prayer going, and you'd better have some Word coming in and going out.

In John 6:63, Jesus said,

"The words that I speak to you they are spirit, and they are life."

The very words that He speaks to us are life. That word "life" there is the word *Zoe*, which is actually the highest and the best that is found in Jesus. It is life as God knows it.

He says the words that He speaks to us are spirit. The first part of this verse says that the flesh profits nothing, but it is the Spirit that gives life. Jesus' words are spirit, so they do profit us, and they give life, *Zoe*.

Do you want the best and the highest that Jesus has already obtained for you? You will never have them unless you have the Word in your life. As the Word comes in, it produces both spirit and life for you. You need both.

Romans 10:17 says,
"So then faith comes by hearing, and hearing by the word of God."

"Hearing" is a continuous and repeated action here—"hearing and hearing and hearing." If you want faith awakened and energized in your life, you must constantly, continuously, and repeatedly be giving your attention to the Word of God.

If your Word level is low, and you are trying to believe God for something, you are deceiving yourself. There is a direct correlation between your Word level and your faith level. If your Word level is low, I guarantee you, your faith level is low.

Whose responsibility is this? In Second Timothy 2:15, the King James Version says,

"*Study to shew thyself approved unto God, a workman that needeth not to be ashamed, rightly dividing the word of truth.*"

Look at Second Timothy 3:16, 17 in the New King James Version. It begins, *"All Scripture is given by inspiration of God."* This literally means that it is God-breathed.

Have you ever written something really profound or poetic? It came out of your heart. Guys, when you were courting your wife, did you ever send her something sweet and romantic? Did you ever come up with a poem? I hope you didn't just steal it from a Hallmark card. If it came out of your heart, it was inspired.

It is saying here that all Scripture comes by the inspiration of God. It literally means that the words of the Bible are God-breathed. They came out of His inspiration. God breathed out the Word of God.

Now look at the rest of it.
>   *"All Scripture is given by inspiration of God, and is profitable for doctrine, for reproof, for correction, for instruction in righteousness,*
>   *that the man of God may be complete, thoroughly equipped for every good work."*

If you don't have the Scripture in your life, your doctrine will be messed up. You'll be badly in need of reproof and correction. You won't have any instruction in righteousness. You won't be complete, and you won't be equipped for every good work. So the key here is having the Word of God in your life.

Ephesians 6:14-17 describes the parts of the armor of God. Notice this: you never take the armor of God off. Some people are consumed with putting it on. Put it on and leave it on.

You don't take off the helmet of salvation or the breastplate of righteousness. You never say, "Oh, I hope the devil doesn't catch me when I have my salvation and righteousness off." No, it's what becomes yours when you put on the new man in Christ. Part of that armor, your only offensive weapon, is *"the sword of the Spirit, which is the word of God."* We must have the Word of God.

Let's look at prayer briefly. In Luke 18:1 Jesus says, *"Men always ought to pray and not lose heart."*

That means not give up. Prayer is vital to us. You cannot just think your way through life. You can't just think about it, and you can't just fill out prayer-request cards.

Now I encourage you to fill out prayer requests. At the same time, pick up a praise-report card, if you are in faith. Then turn in the prayer request and keep your praise-report card ready. Now you're waiting to fill it out, instead of thinking, "Well, I wonder what will happen."

You need to believe God, and prayer needs to be a vital part of your life. Don't just think about it, don't just fill out something, don't just share your need with others—*you* pray about it.

Jesus said that if you're not praying, then you are going to lose heart. Have you ever felt like giving up? Pray!

"I didn't feel like praying." You cannot ignore some warnings on your spiritual dashboard.

First Thessalonians 5:17 says that we are to *"pray without ceasing."* In Ephesians 6:18 we are to pray always, with all types of prayer in the Spirit. We are to have prayer in our lives constantly.

Jude 20 in the Amplified Bible says this.

"But you, beloved, build yourselves up [founded] on your most holy faith, [make progress, rise like an edifice higher and higher], praying in the Holy Spirit."

You will actually be building your faith and building your spirit man by praying in the Spirit.

We need to have prayer constantly. We need to have the Word constantly. Prayer is you communicating with God. The Word is God communicating with you. If you have prayer, and you have the Word, you will have strong faith, and you will have a key for preservation and increase.

16
Do You Understand?

The fourteenth key is *understanding*. Now remember these are keys. Don't you hate it when you lose your keys? You can't go anywhere. You can't do anything.

One morning, getting ready for work, I couldn't find my keys. I looked everywhere. My car was sitting right there, but I couldn't go anywhere.

My wife said, "Take my key for your car."

"No, I need my keys. I have to get in my office. I need the key to my desk. I have to find my keys." We cannot live life, certainly not in preservation and increase, without our keys.

Proverbs 24:3, 4 reads,

"Through wisdom a house is built, And by understanding it is established; By knowledge the rooms are filled With all precious and pleasant riches."

The Amplified Bible says,

"Through skillful and godly Wisdom is a house (a life, a home, a family) built, and by understanding it is established [on a sound and good foundation]."

If you are going to have preservation and increase, you must have a strong foundation. Your life, your family, your home, your business, your ministry—everything—must be built on a solid base. The way that is done is by understanding the things of God.

It is not so much a mental understanding. That is where a lot of people miss out. What is needed is a spiritual understanding. You must have a mental understanding, though, because that becomes the "handle" that you retrieve it with.

There are times that I have been praying, waiting on God, and studying the Word, and I will get revelation—spiritual understanding—on something.

I'll come out of my room and say to my wife, "Oh, Alicia, I just got something."

She'll say "What is it?"

And I'll say, "I just can't put it in words yet."

Do you know what you have to do? You have to sit with it for a while. You have to meditate on it, and you can't even put it over in words yet, but it is down in your heart.

Sometimes you're alone with God, and something will just drop down in there. You'll cry, you'll rejoice, you'll get all excited about it, but you can't get it out yet. But stay with it, and finally you'll get a handle on it. You see, you eventually understand spiritual revelation with your mind, too.

There are different things that you understand. For instance, what kind of peace has He given us? He has given us great peace, and He has given us perfect peace. What about that peace? It guards our hearts, and it guards our minds. And, notice, it passes understanding.

We might know all this in our mental understanding, but we also know it down in our hearts. If it is really real in your life, you know it in your heart as much as you know it in your head, or more. What you know up in your head is just the handle, so that you can retrieve it.

When you have that revelation of peace in your heart, you have to be able to retrieve it, and you need to be able to confess it over your life. So we must mostly have a spiritual understanding, but it is important that we have a mental understanding.

In First Corinthians 2:14 the Amplified Bible says—

But the natural, nonspiritual man does not accept or welcome or admit into his heart the gifts and teachings and revelations of the Spirit of God, for they are folly (meaningless nonsense) to him; and he is incapable of knowing them (of progressively recognizing, understanding, and becoming better acquainted with them) because they are spiritually discerned and estimated and appreciated.

With your natural mind alone, you cannot capture the revelation and the understanding of the things of God. Some people know spiritual or religious jargon, because they've read books. Those books are the revelation someone else received from God. Then these people read the book and get only the handle, but not the revelation.

In high school, I wanted to have a citizens' band radio, and my step-dad said, "No, you don't need a CB radio." A friend of mine gave me a magnetic antenna so I looked like I had a CB radio.

My friends would say, "Hey, what's your 'handle'?"

"Bugle Boy." And I didn't know anything about CB's. "Hey, where's your radio?"

"It's in the shop." You see, it forces you to lie, when you don't have the goods. I had the antenna, though. It looked like I was Joe CB, but I wasn't.

If you only have the handle, and you can talk the talk, but you don't have it down here in your spirit, it won't do you much good. So if you are trying to understand these things, you must wait on God.

There is no such thing as a "microwave" spiritual walk with God. If the things of God were instant, then people of no character would possess them. Anybody could just come in and get them. But there is a waiting period.

God is saying, "Hey, this is a precious thing. You wait here, and I will pour it into your life." If you just run in and grab, you won't get it. That's why you have to wait upon God.

You won't get the real understanding in your head first. You might get a concept, but you won't get the revelation there. In your head is where you get the handle. This spiritual understanding is a knowing, down in your spirit man. Then, in your mind, you can understand the concept of that revelation. That is how you're able to retrieve it.

In Mark 4:3-9 Jesus is teaching about being receptive.
"Listen! Behold, a sower went out to sow.

> *"And it happened, as he sowed, that some seed fell by the wayside; and the birds of the air came and devoured it.*
>
> *"Some fell on stony ground, where it did not have much earth; and immediately it sprang up because it had no depth of earth.*
>
> *"But when the sun was up it was scorched, and because it had no root it withered away.*
>
> *"And some seed fell among thorns; and the thorns grew up and choked it, and it yielded no crop.*
>
> *"But other seed fell on good ground and yielded a crop that sprang up, increased and produced: some thirtyfold, some sixty, and some a hundred."*
>
> *And He said to them, "He who has ears to hear, let him hear."*

That word *hear* means "understand." He who is ready to understand, let him understand.

The disciples ask Him then for the meaning.

> *"And He said to them, 'Do you not understand this parable? How then will you understand all the parables?'"*

He is saying, "If you don't get understanding of this parable, you are going to miss it completely." In verses 14 and 15, Jesus begins to explain it.

> *"The sower sows the word.*
>
> *"And these are the ones by the wayside where the word is sown. When they hear, Satan comes immediately and takes away the word that was sown in their hearts."*

The most important understanding is in your spirit man. But we must have a mental understanding as well, because that is how we have a grip on it. That concept of it is enough to let us pull up the revelation that is literally in spirit words. If you don't get understanding both in your heart and in your mind, you will lose it.

My ministry gift is to teach, and as a teacher I am to get it across in a clear, concise, and digestible manner so that people can understand it in their minds. However, when I was in algebra class in school, I had information without understanding. Therefore, I didn't have knowledge, so there was no way I could have wisdom on how to apply the information. It couldn't possibly stay with me.

Understanding is key. That is why you must make sure that when you read the scriptures, you don't just run right over them. Take the time, slow down, and seek some understanding .

"Well," you say, "my spirit is getting it." Your spirit already had it. You need to take hold of it with your mental understanding.

Notice in the parable the Word was sown in their hearts, but they lost it. How did they lose it? It said that Satan came immediately to snatch it away.

In verses 23-25, Jesus urges them again to press in.
"If anyone has ears to hear, let him hear."
Then He said to them, "Take heed what you hear. With the same measure you use, it will be measured to you; and to you who hear, more will be given.
"For whoever has, to him more will be given; but whoever does not have, even what he has will be taken away from him."

Let me paraphrase. We know from the last chapter that the Word is spirit, it is life, it causes faith to come, and you need the

Word. Jesus has said that when the Word is sown in your heart, you must have understanding in order to keep it.

Jesus goes on to say that you must take heed—pay careful attention—to what you hear, so that you will understand. That's because if you have understanding, more revelation will be given to you. However, if you don't have understanding, you will lose even what you have.

You have a responsibility. You need to understand that you need to understand. But how can you develop your understanding?

Psalm 119:130 in the Amplified Bible says,

"The entrance and unfolding of Your words give light; their unfolding gives understanding (discernment and comprehension) to the simple."

The Word of God is the language of the Spirit of God, and the Spirit will bring you understanding and revelation. I heard one minister put it this way. Imagine a typewriter for communicating with the Spirit. If all you know how to type is "JKL, JKL, JKL," and that's all you can read, it's hard to communicate with anybody. Even if someone writes you a whole letter back, using all the keys, it doesn't mean anything to you if you understand only "JKL."

What we need to do is understand the language of the Spirit. The more you learn of the Word of God, the more that the Spirit of God can communicate with you.

Some of us just have that little "JKL, JKL," and we wonder why we can't get any real revelation from the Spirit of God. You need to expand your vocabulary. How do you do that? The language of the Spirit is the Word of God, and it is the Word of God that the Spirit will use to give you understanding.

Paul prayed for the believers to grow in understanding. Colossians 1:9 reads,

"[We] ask that you may be filled with the knowledge of His will in all wisdom and spiritual understanding."

In Ephesians 1:16-18 he wrote—

[I] do not cease to give thanks for you, making mention of you in my prayers:

that the God of our Lord Jesus Christ, the Father of glory, may give to you the spirit of wisdom and revelation in the knowledge of Him,

the eyes of your understanding being enlightened; that you may know what is the hope of His calling, what are the riches of the glory of His inheritance in the saints.

Once you get understanding, once the eyes of your understanding have been enlightened, then you can know the hope of your calling. That is an important point that you need to *understand*.

17
Get Over It

K ey No. 15 is *quick recovery*. My next statement probably won't bless you very much upon initial impact. But trust that I am saying it in love, and it is truth. *Maturity is measured by recovery time.*

How long does it take you to recover? If you get bad news, how long does it take you to recover? If you mess up, how long does it take you to recover? Your maturity is measured by your recovery time.

Proverbs 24:16 reads,

"For a righteous man may fall seven times and rise again, but the wicked shall fall by calamity."

The fact that you are a righteous man or woman doesn't mean you won't fall.

When we looked at adding to your faith, we saw that the first chapter of Second Peter tells you how not to fall. If you will do exactly what it says in Second Peter 1:2-12, you will not stumble or fall, guaranteed.

Jude 24 says that Jesus is able to present you spotless and blameless before the throne of God. He is able to keep you from stumbling or falling. In Jesus, in the Word of God, through the

Holy Spirit, there is the provision that you can go through this life and not fall and not stumble.

Now, this is not just about falling down physically. We are talking about a spiritual concept here—about avoiding the danger of falling spiritually.

"Well, what do you mean by falling spiritually?" you may say. "I'm not going to rob a bank. I'm not going to get into adultery. I'm not going to do whatever."

You fall in other ways. What about when you let your emotions take over? What about saying something you later regret? What about getting offended and carrying a bad attitude? You have fallen. When you do that, your maturity is measured by what? By your recovery time.

So if a righteous man falls, and even if he falls seven times, he will still get back up.

Micah 7:8 says,
   "Do not rejoice over me, my enemy; When I fall, I will arise."

Read that again. You need to have that in your heart.

You aren't planning on falling, but if and when you would fall, declare, "Enemy, don't you rejoice over me, because I am getting right back up." We need to have this resolve in our hearts: "If I do go down, I guarantee you I am getting back up, and I am coming back at you harder than before."

Stir yourself. There needs to be that in you, that if you fall, you are quick to recover.

Too many believers are lying down. Satan has them out of the game. You ask them what they're doing there.

"I got knocked down."

"Well, get up."

"But somebody said something to me."

"Well, get up."

"I went back and sinned again." That's like Proverbs 26:11. *"As a dog returns to his own vomit, So a fool repeats his folly."*

Tell yourself, "Get up!" You have to be determined. You're not staying down. This may be the one-bizillionth time that you have fallen, but you can get back up!

Is it only weak people who fall? Look at Psalm 37:23, 24.
The steps of a good man are ordered by the Lord, And He delights in his way.
Though he fall, he shall not be utterly cast down; For the Lord upholds him with His hand.

It says, "the steps of a good man." That word for *man* carries with it the idea of "strength," but it has no gender. This good man is strong, but he fell. It could be a woman who is strong.

The steps of those who are strong are ordered by the Lord. The Amplified Bible says the Lord *"busies Himself with his every step."* Did you know that God is busying Himself with your every step? That's good news.

But verse 24 says, "though he fall." We have watched some very strong ones fall. Then we think, "Well, I'm nothing, so I am sure to fall."

No, no, no, no. You are stronger probably than many are. It is time to build some confidence in the Body of Christ.

You say, "I thought he was a faithful man. And look, he yelled at somebody." A faithful man who falls will be faithful to repent. He doesn't stay down.

Remember this, too. No matter who falls, Jesus is still worthy to be followed.

Now it says that if this strong one falls, he will not be cast down. *Fall* there means to fail or to stumble. It can be caused by yourself, it can be caused by others, it can be caused by your enemy, or it can be caused by your circumstances.

You don't have to stay there. It says you will not be utterly *cast down*, that is "to perish, cease, or be finished." It's not the end.

Continuing with verse 24, it says, *"...For the Lord upholds him with His hand."*

In the Hebrew, *uphold* means "to bear up, to take hold of, to sustain." The Lord will bear you up, take hold of you, and sustain you. With what? With His hand.

186

Hand throughout Scripture symbolizes His power. The Hebrew word here actually means an open hand. Though you fall, He doesn't stand over you, fold His arms, and look at you in disgust. He doesn't step on you and walk off.

Do you know what He does? He reaches down with the open hand of His power, takes hold, lifts up, sustains. So you have no reason to stay down. You have to get back up.

Jesus is waiting right there to help you back up with the open hand of His power. Get it under the Blood and get going! No matter how small or how big a deal you think it was, if you fell, don't stay down there. Have a quick recovery.

You see, if you just lie there, you will end up tripping somebody else. Let me illustrate. Others are watching you. You've been an example and an encouragement to them. Now they come along the path, and they see you lying down.

"What's wrong with you?"

"I fell. It doesn't work."

Before you know it, they are falling right over you. So a quick recovery is vital for their sake, too.

If you stay down there, the devil will go ahead and frame you in, cover you over, and plant poison ivy on top of you. Don't stay down. Make that quick recovery. Make your confession, "I'm either up or I'm getting up!"

18
It Pays to Obey

The sixteenth and last key is *severe obedience.*

I didn't say *convenient* obedience. Have you ever had convenient obedience? "Oh, this is a perfect opportunity to be obedient." No, we're talking about severe obedience, if you are going to play for keeps.

Hebrews 10:36 in the Amplified Bible reads,
   "For you have need of steadfast patience and endurance, so that you may perform and fully accomplish the will of God, and thus receive and carry away [and enjoy to the full] what is promised."

You need patience, so that after that you've done the will of God, you may receive what He promised. This means those promises are conditional.

The Lord has spoken to my heart time and time again, "You know, I can't take you any further until you do what I have already told you to do."

My children are this way sometimes. I say, "Hey, kids, we are going to go to such and such. But before we do that, you've got to clean your room."

So they will move one or two toys. Or they will fall down on the floor and say, "We're too tired."

"Well, then you're too tired to go anywhere."

"No, no, no, we'll do it."

"But, Daddy, I didn't make all this mess. He helped me." You know you can make a million excuses, and you'll never get anywhere. What do you have to do? You have to fulfill the condition. You can't go further until you obey the first things.

What has God told you to do? You already know the simple things to do. Maybe you're asking God to work in a relationship, but you won't forgive. God says, "I can't do anything until you do your part."

"God, please work in my finances." You know to give, but you won't give.

What can God do? You have to obey in the little things.
In John 14:15 Jesus said, ***"If you love Me, keep my commandments."*** What He saying is "If you really love Me, obey Me." Severe obedience.

Obedience is not motivated by fear. Obedience is motivated by love. Because I love God, I will obey God. Now you can call that the fear of the Lord. That's because the fear of the Lord is that my greatest dread is to disappoint Him.

So it is a severe obedience. It's not because He is waiting for you to mess up, so he can squish you or flick you. No, God's not looking to do that. God's looking to bless you.

Out of the motivation of your love for Him, you obey. Don't obey God only so you won't get caught doing wrong. If that's the only reason you obey, you are just as guilty as if you disobeyed. If the only reason I don't rob stores in my town is because they'll recognize me, I'm not quite getting the message here.

Your obedience even in little things should come out of this desire and love for God that causes you just to want to please Him.

How does this apply to preservation and increase? Deuteronomy 28:1 says—

Now it shall come to pass, if you diligently obey the voice of the Lord your God, to observe carefully all His commandments which I command you today, that the Lord your God will set you high above all nations of the earth."

Deuteronomy 29:9 adds,

"Therefore keep the words of this covenant, and do them, that you may prosper in all that you do."

And look at Joshua 1:7, 8.

Only be strong and very courageous, that you may observe to do according to all the law which Moses My servant commanded you; do not turn from it to the right hand or to the left, that you may prosper wherever you go.

This Book of the Law shall not depart from your mouth, but you shall meditate in it day and night, that you may observe to do according to all that is written in it. For then you will make your way prosperous, and then you will have good success."

If you want blessings, if you want increase, if you want preservation, if you want prosperity in your life, you have to observe to *do*. You have to observe to do—carefully, diligently—all that He has commanded you to do.

Now, you need to be careful here. There are some people who are "religiously robotic," because they are trying to do all the law. Praise God that we are under grace. I want to tell you how to do it.

Look at Galatians 5:14. ***"For all the law is fulfilled in one word, even in this: 'You shall love your neighbor as yourself.'"*** Do you know what the bottom line is? Walk in love.

"But they're being mean to me." Love never fails. Walk in love.

"They're trying to destroy me." Love never fails. Walk in love. One step outside of love is sin.

"How do I monitor this? How am I going to fulfill all the law?"

You can't fulfill all the law. If we could have fulfilled all the law, Jesus never would have had to come. You can't fulfill all the law.

"So what do I do?" All the law is fulfilled in this one saying, this one word: love your neighbor as yourself. Walk in love. Love never fails, in any relationship, in any situation. If you will walk in love, and you give that your severe attention, you are going to obey God.

Why do you obey God? Because you love Him. Why do you bear with one another? Because you love them. Where do you get that love? God shed that love abroad in your heart by the Holy Ghost. (Rom. 5:5.)

We have to walk in a severe obedience. Let's get practical here for just a moment. There are little things in your life that at first glance don't look like they have much to do with love. They are little things that God has already told you to do.

Some of you men need to serve your wives in ways that God will show you. Some of you men need to take the spiritual headship of your home, to go pray with your wives and your children and lead them in the Word. You know to do that. God has already put that in your heart.

You may be longing for peace in your home. Isaiah 54:13 says, *"All your children shall be taught by the Lord, And great shall be the peace of your children."*

My wife and I on occasion have asked ourselves, "What is wrong with these kids?" We have to stop and look sometimes. If our schedule has started to lord over us, then they're not being taught by the Lord from the best source that He has given them, and that is Mom and Dad.

You may be wondering why things aren't happening quite right, or why some things are slipping out of your life. You need to get back to severe obedience. God has told you some things already. You know some simple little things that you have to do.

"Well, what difference is that going to make?" You already see the difference your disobedience is making. Get back to those things. For example, God has put on your heart to forgive some people, and you haven't done it yet. You need to do it. It's severe obedience.

This is a major key in holding on to the things of God. Do you want to play for keeps? Do you want the things of God to continue and expand in your life?

These are the keys to preservation and increase.
- Be thankful
- Listen
- Walk in wisdom
- Leave no openings
- Be single-minded
- Sow
- Be willing to be misunderstood
- Add to your faith
- Be fearless
- Have faithfulness
- Confess your belief
- Apply the Blood
- Watch your Word and prayer levels
- Seek understanding
- Make a quick recovery
- Practice severe obedience

Now I am mindful that there may be at least several dozen more keys in the scriptures. But these are the ones that God has laid on my heart. Get into these. Study these. Don't just hear these things and go unchanged. Get these keys!

If you knew that this works—and it works—and if you had any hope these things might bring preservation and increase in your life, you'd be a fool not to spend the time and effort to add these keys to your spiritual key ring.

Get these things in your life and apply them to your life, and in the doing you will be blessed! You can experience *preservation and increase as you learn to play for keeps!*

Pray this prayer to make
Jesus the Lord of your life!

Father God, I come to you in Jesus' Name. I realize my need for you in my life. The Bible says in Romans 10:13 that "whoever calls upon the name of the Lord shall be saved." So I call on you now and I ask you to come into my life to be my Savior and my Lord. Forgive my sins and cleanse me from all unrighteousness.

I believe in my heart that Jesus died for me and that God raised Him from the dead. I confess that Jesus is Lord and now I am saved! (Romans 10:9-10)

Fill me with your peace, your joy and with the assurance that you will never leave me or forsake me. Help me now to grow in my Christian life.

I'm saved. I'm born-again. I'm a new creature. I belong to YOU! Thank you, Lord!

In Jesus' Name...Amen.

To order additional copies of *Playing For Keeps*, complete the information below.

Ship to: (please print)

Name _____

Address _____

City, State, Zip _____

Daytime Phone _____

_____copies of *Playing For Keeps* @ $ 9.99 each $ _____

Postage and handling @ $ 2.50 per book $ _____

Florida residents add 6% tax $ _____

Total amount enclosed $ _____

<u>Make checks payable to Ocala Word of Faith Church.</u>

Send to:
**Ocala Word of Faith Church
Dept. PFK
4741 S.W. 20th Street
Ocala, FL 34474**